MAXnotes

*Toni Morrison's*

# Song of Solomon

*Text by*
**Nancy A. Ciabattari**
*(M.A., Brown University)*
Slavic Department
Brown University
Providence, Rhode Island

*Illustrations by*
**Ann Tango-Schurmann**

*Research & Education Association*

# What **MAXnotes®** *Will Do for You*

This book is intended to help you absorb the essential contents and features of Toni Morrison's *Song of Solomon* and to help you gain a thorough understanding of the work. The book has been designed to do this more quickly and effectively than any other study guide.

For best results, this **MAXnotes** book should be used as a companion to the actual work, not instead of it. The interaction between the two will greatly benefit you.

To help you in your studies, this book presents the most up-to-date interpretations of every section of the actual work, followed by questions and fully explained answers that will enable you to analyze the material critically. The questions also will help you to test your understanding of the work and will prepare you for discussions and exams.

Meaningful illustrations are included to further enhance your understanding and enjoyment of the literary work. The illustrations are designed to place you into the mood and spirit of the work's settings.

The **MAXnotes** also include summaries, character lists, explanations of plot, and section-by-section analyses. A biography of the author and discussion of the work's historical context will help you put this literary piece into the proper perspective of what is taking place.

The use of this study guide will save you the hours of preparation time that would ordinarily be required to arrive at a complete grasp of this work of literature. You will be well prepared for classroom discussions, homework, and exams. The guidelines that are included for writing papers and reports on various topics will prepare you for any added work which may be assigned.

The **MAXnotes** will take your grades "to the max."

Dr. Max Fogiel
Program Director

# Contents

---

**Each chapter includes List of Characters, Summary, Analysis, Study Questions and Answers, and Suggested Essay Topics.**

---

*v*

# SECTION ONE

# *Introduction*

### *The Life and Work of Toni Morrison*

Toni Morrison was born Chloe AnthonyWofford on February 18, 1931 in Lorain, Ohio, the second of four children of George Wofford, a shipyard welder, and Ramah Willis Wofford. Morrison recalls a childhood filled with singing and oral storytelling. While Morrison was an avid reader of the great Russian writers, *Madame Bovary*, and Jane Austen, she also vividly remembers the African folklore and myths that were an integral part of her youth.

Morrison refers to the oral storytelling in her household as "a spoken library." She describes it as "children's stories my family told, spirituals, the ghost stories, the blues, and folk tales and myths, and the everyday...." Morrison "wanted to write out of the matrix of memory, of recollection, and to approximate the sensual and visceral responses (she) had to the world (she) lived in...." From this she wanted "to recreate the civilization of black people...the manners, judgments, values, morals...." (Morrison, 29)

Born into the Depression era, in a multicultural town near Cleveland, Morrison was exposed to the struggling masses who often went hungry. She was also exposed to the injustices of racism, although she had many white friends as a child. Morrison tells of her mother battling segregation by refusing to sit in the "colored" section on public buses. Morrison's father "received shocking impressions of adult white people" while growing up in Georgia, and the bitterness never left him. (Strouse, 53)

Morrison completed high school at the top of her class and attended Howard University in Washington, D.C. Upon entering college, she changed her name to "Toni." While at Howard, she joined the Howard University Players, a repertory troupe, and toured the Deep South during several summers. "...Seeing its roads, its shotgun houses, its schools, its particular brand of segregation" left a deep impression on her. "Seeing first-hand what life was like for Southern blacks in the late 1940s and early 1950s" made the stories Morrison had heard her parents tell about the hardships of their lives in the South more tangible. Morrison's maternal grandfather, John Solomon Willis, "had been cheated out of his 88 acres of Alabama land, land legally granted to his Indian mother by the U.S. government following the Civil War." (Century, 33–35)

Morrison graduated with a B.A. in English in 1953. She completed an M.A. in English from Cornell in 1955.

Morrison taught at Texas Southern University for two years before returning to teach at Howard. Morrison's presence at Howard was important for her growing social consciousness. In 1957, the civil rights movement was just beginning. Living in the nation's capital and teaching at one of the most prestigious black colleges in the country, Morrison was exposed to many key black figures in the civil rights movement. Among others, she knew Leroi Jones (Amiri Baraka), the radical black poet and had Claude Brown (the future author of *Manchild in the Promised Land*) as one of her students. Another student, Stokely Carmichael, the future leader of the Student Nonviolent Coordinating Committee became "one of the most vocal advocates of the Black Power movement." (Century, 37)

In 1957, Morrison married Jamaican architect Harold Morrison. They were divorced in 1964, but not before having two sons.

In 1965, Morrison entered publishing. She worked first as an editor at Random House, in the Syracuse office, and subsequently was promoted to a senior editor in the New York office, where she worked until 1983. While at Random House, she edited works by Muhammad Ali, Toni Cade Bambara, Angela Davis, and many other important black writers. She also worked on *The Black Book*, a compilation of slave narratives, news clippings, advertisements, and photographs that records three centuries of black history.

In 1989, after having taught at the State University at Purchase and at Albany, Bard College, Yale, and Rutgers, Morrison accepted an endowed professorship at Princeton University. She was the first black woman to receive such an honor.

Her first novel, the critically acclaimed *The Bluest Eye* (1970) deals with the issue of racism and its impact on young black girls growing up poor in Ohio. The novel centers around Pecola Breedlove, a little black girl who believes that she can right all the wrongs of her world if only she can have blue eyes. A major theme of the novel, and of subsequent novels by Toni Morrison, is the difficulty of maintaining a secure black identity in a world where the larger society conspires against that identity. Critic Jean Strouse adeptly points out the parallels between Pecola Breedlove's conflict and that of African-Americans historically by drawing an analogy with W.E.B. Du Bois's work *The Souls of Black Folk*. Du Bois speaks of a "double consciousness" by which the African-American constantly experiences "this sense of always looking at one's self through the eyes of others, of measuring one's soul by the tape of a world that looks on in amused contempt and pity. One ever feels his twoness—an American, a Negro; two souls, two thoughts, two unreconciled strivings; two warring ideas in one dark body, whose dogged strength alone keeps it from being torn asunder." (Strouse, 54)

*The Bluest Eye* was followed by *Sula* (1974), a novel about the friendship of Sula Peace and Nel Wright and their attempt to re-create themselves because "they were neither white nor male, and that (therefore) all freedom and triumph was forbidden to them...." Morrison's third novel, *Song of Solomon* (1977) was a bestseller, and her first novel in which the protagonist was male. Susan Lardner describes the novel as "a domestic epic—a rhapsodic work, demonstrating the virtues of the spoken word and the abiding presence in certain corners of the world of a lively oral tradition." (Lardner, 217) Morrison believes it is important for black culture to know that it has "a legitimate source of language." Morrison emphasizes that black culture is "most accessible in the language, the structure, the sound, what people call slang, the metaphors, the similes, the paradoxes, the ironies...."(Morrison, 29)

It is Morrison's ability to convey this language both in her narratives and the dialogues of her characters that gives her work its strong expressive powers. Morrison describes language as "the thing that black people love so much—the saying of words, holding them on the tongue, experimenting with them, playing with them. It's a love, a passion. Its function is like a preacher's; to make you stand up out of your seat, make you lose yourself and hear yourself. The worst of all possible things that could happen (to black people) would be to lose that language." (LeClair, 27)

The African-American male writers who preceded Morrison—such as Richard Wright, Ralph Ellison, and James Baldwin—wrote about the problems of being a black man in a white society. The "black power" advocates of the 1960s such as Stokely Carmichael and Leroi Jones wrote "...books and political slogans about power...addressed to white men trying to explain or prove something to them." Morrison explains that "The fight was between men, for king of the hill." (Strouse, 55)

The voices of African-American women writers, and Toni Morrison in particular, have a different focal point than their male counterparts. Their intention, first and foremost, is to address the black community. Toni Morrison categorizes her fiction as "village literature." Morrison writes fiction "for my people, which is necessary and legitimate but which also allows me to get in touch with all sorts of people." Morrison believes that writing is an act "to give nourishment" to her readers. Rather than accept the new "urban values," Morrison looks to restore the "old values" and "the language that black people spoke to its original power." (LeClair, 26) Morrison, like Alice Walker, Toni Cade Bambara, and other African-American women writers, uses black oral history, myth, and folklore to restore black culture's heritage.

In 1980, among other honors, President Jimmy Carter appointed Morrison to the National Council on the Arts.

Morrison's fourth novel, *Tar Baby* was published in 1981. Seven years later, she was awarded the Pulitzer Prize for her novel on slavery, *Beloved* (1987). Her next novel, *Jazz*, appeared in 1992.

In 1993, Morrison was the first African-American to win the coveted Nobel Prize in Literature for a body of work that is now internationally recognized for its high literary quality, its concern with moral issues, and its depth of imagination.

### *Historical Background*

Historically, the time period of *Song of Solomon* parallels the era in which Toni Morrison has lived. The novel begins on Morrison's birthdate. It is the era of the Great Depression, with its disastrous economic effect on the daily lives of Americans.

Both Morrison and the characters of *Song of Solomon* experience the effects of segregation and racism in their lives in the 1930s. Morrison documents historic events and interweaves them with fictional ones. For example, the government in the 1930s continued to uphold the Fifteenth Amendment to the Constitution, which condoned "separate but equal" institutions for black and white people. But in *Song of Solomon*, "(No) Mercy Hospital" excludes blacks, and there is no other hospital provided for them.

In *Song of Solomon*, the author allows the reader to "bear witness" to historical events by using fictitious characters. She then lets the reader draw his or her own conclusions.

Much of the novel takes place in the 1950s and 1960s. Historically, this is the era of the civil rights movement. Morrison refers to dates during this time period to better explain the behavior of her characters.

The lynching of Emmett Till, in 1955, is one such date. In 1954, the doctrine of "separate but equal" had been overturned by the Supreme Court, and the angry killing of Emmett Till was an indirect reaction to the Court's new ruling. In this way, history informs the behavior of the characters in *Song of Solomon* .

Milkman's best friend, Guitar, becomes a member of the radical group the Seven Days as a reaction to the black man's plight in the 1950s. Near the novel's end, 1963, there is much evidence of heightened frustration in the African-American community. Historically, many followers of Martin Luther King, Jr. were becoming disenchanted with the lack of progress in social change that Dr. King attempted to forge through nonviolent means. The character of Guitar Bains reflects this frustration. Bains appears to subscribe to an activism similar to that of Malcolm X, a follower of Elijah Mohammad's Nation of Islam. As 1963 draws to a close, many African-Americans began to embrace the Nation of Islam's more militant approach and its call for racial separatism.

The Book-of-the-Month Club advertised *Song of Solomon* as

one of its main selections in 1977, referring to it as "the best novel of the black experience since (Ralph Ellison's) *Invisible Man.*" The best-seller was honored with several distinguished awards, including the prestigious National Book Critics' Circle Award in 1978. Following the success of *Song of Solomon*, Morrison was featured on the cover of *Newsweek.* She was invited to do a PBS series called *Writers in America*, and was interviewed on *The Dick Cavett Show.*

*Song of Solomon* was compared by the general public and some critics to Alex Haley's *Roots* because of its similar plot, the search for an African-American family's ancestral roots, dating back to slavehood. However, *Time* magazine condemned the comparison, saying that *Song of Solomon*, unlike *Roots*, has "an artistic vision that encompasses both a private and a national heritage...any comparison (with *Roots*) must end with the superior quality of Morrison's imagination and prose." (Wigan, 76)

At the time of its publication, Morrison's novel was her strongest statement to date on white society's oppression of African-Americans. However, critics agreed that although the novel "might easily be considered anti-white," that "the author's perceptions are human, rather than racist, and whites who read her will feel something—will live something—of what it means to be born black in America." (Millar, 25)

### Master List of Characters

**Robert Smith**—*life insurance agent and member of the Seven Days organization. He attempts to fly in the first chapter.*

**Dr. Foster**—*father of Ruth Dead, and the only colored doctor in the city until he died in 1921. "Not Doctor Street" is named after him.*

**Ruth Dead**—*Milkman's mother, Macon's wife, and Dr. Foster's daughter; she is the first "colored" woman to give birth at Mercy Hospital. She is born in 1901. Her name in Hebrew means "companion."*

**First Corinthians (Corinthians)**—*Milkman's older sister; she is 13 years older than her brother. She is the lover of Henry Porter. As is the tradition for Dead family women, her name is chosen randomly from the Bible at her birth. Her name refers to a book of the New Testament, the first epistle addressed by St. Paul to the*

*Christians in the ancient Greek city of Corinth. Ironically, Corinth was known as a city of ill-repute for its sexual promiscuity, while the character Corinthians is a virgin throughout much of* Song of Solomon.

**Magdalene (Lena)**—*Milkman's oldest sister, she is 14 years older than her brother. Her name is arbitrarily chosen from the Bible and refers to the reformed prostitute that Jesus cures of evil spirits in the Book of Luke (New Testament).*

**Pilate Dead**—*Milkman's aunt and spiritual mother; she is Macon Dead's sister and the mother of the illegitimate Reba and grandmother of Hagar. Pilate's name is arbitrarily chosen by her father from the Bible. Because he can't read, her father chooses the name because it "looked like a tree hanging in some princely but protective way over a row of smaller trees." Ironically in the Bible (New Testament: Book of Matthew), Pilate is the last name of a man, a Roman official (the procurator of Judea) who authorized the execution of Jesus Christ.*

**Freddy**—*the Dead family's tenant, a janitor, and the originator of Milkman's nickname; he is often referred to as "gold-toothed."*

**Mrs. Bains**—*referred to as "the stout woman" in the first chapter. She is Guitar Bains' grandmother.*

**Cency**—*Guitar Bains' mother and Mrs. Bains' daughter.*

**Guitar Bains**—*Milkman's best friend and member of the Seven Days.*

**Macon Dead III (Milkman)**—*protagonist of the novel; he is the only son of Macon and Ruth Dead. He is born in 1931.*

**Macon Dead II or Jr.**—*Milkman's father and Ruth's husband; he is born in 1891. He is a successful man of property.*

**Circe**—*the midwife who delivers Macon and is present when Pilate "births" herself. She conceals them after Macon Dead I is killed and supplies Milkman with his family history. Circe's name derives from Greek mythology. According to myth, she is a beautiful enchantress known for her magic arts and the daughter of Helios—the Sun God. In the Greek epic, Homer's* Odyssey, *Circe detains Odysseus for a year and turns his men into swine.*

**Henry Porter**—*Macon Dead's tenant and a member of the Seven Days He is Corinthians' lover.*

**Reba Dead (Rebecca or Rebekah)**—*the illegitimate daughter of Pilate Dead, she is Milkman's aunt, and the mother of the illegitimate Hagar. Her name derives from the Bible: Rebecca or Rebekah is the wife of Isaac, a Hebrew patriarch. (Book of Genesis)*

**Hagar Dead**—*the illegitimate daughter of Reba, she is the granddaughter of Pilate Dead. Hagar is Milkman's cousin and lover. In the Bible, Hagar refers to the concubine of Abraham (the first patriarch and progenitor of the Hebrews). The biblical Hagar is Abraham's wife, Sarah's handmaiden; Hagar is the mother of Abraham's illegitimate son Ishmael and is cast aside by Abraham; her name means "forsaken." (Book of Genesis)*

**Macon Dead I**—*referred to early in the novel only as "Macon's father," he is the member of the family who was misnamed Dead and lost the original family name. His real name is Jake.*

**Feather**—*he is the pool hall owner in the crime-riddled section of town called the Blood Bank.*

**Railroad Tommy**—*one of the owners of the barber shop on Tenth Street and a member of the Seven Days.*

**Hospital Tommy**—*one of the owners of the barber shop and a member of the Seven Days.*

**Anna Djvorak**—*she is the Hungarian woman who credits Dr. Foster with saving her son's life in 1903. Ruth Dead comes to her granddaughter's wedding.*

**Father Padrew**—*the Catholic priest who presides over Mrs. Djvorak's granddaughter's marriage, and who gives communion to Ruth Dead.*

**Empire State**—*he is a Seven Days member who kills a white boy in a school yard after the historic figure Emmett Till is lynched.*

**Mary**—*the barmaid and part-time owner of a bar in the Blood Bank, where Milkman and Guitar often go to drink.*

**Emmett Till**—*a 14-year-old black boy killed in Mississippi in 1955* *for whistling at a white woman. The lynching of this historic figure lives on as a symbol of the racial injustice African-Americans encountered in the 1950s. The men at Tommy's Barbershop discuss Till's lynching, which is avenged by the Seven Days.*

**Winnie Ruth Judd**—*a convicted murderess. The blacks in the novel consider this white woman to be an example of "white madness."*

**Seven Days**—*an activist organization of seven black men who avenge innocent black deaths by randomly killing whites under similar circumstances.*

**Uncle Billy**—*Guitar's uncle, who comes to Michigan from Florida to raise Guitar after his father dies.*

**Moon**—*aids Guitar in preventing Hagar from killing Milkman.*

**Preacher**—*head of family that took the orphaned Pilate in after she decided to leave Pennsylvania to look for her extended family in Virginia.*

**Pickers**—*Migrants Pilate lived and worked with for three years in New York State until they discovered she had no navel.*

**Father of Reba**—*Pilate's lover on an island of black families in Virginia.*

**Michael-Mary Graham**—*the hack-poetess who Corinthians keeps house for.*

**Mr. Solomon**—*name of imaginary husband invented by Pilate to explain to the police whose bones are in the green sack Milkman and Guitar steal from Pilate's house. Not to be confused with the Solomons from Shalimar, Virginia.*

**Nero**—*member of the Seven Days who Milkman sees in Porter's Oldsmobile when Milkman discovers Porter is a member of the Seven Days.*

**Reverend Cooper**—*the Reverend of Danville, Pennsylvania, who Milkman goes to visit to learn about his family. Milkman finds out information about where the cave Pilate and Macon lived in is located from the Reverend.*

**Esther Cooper**—*Reverend Cooper's wife.*

**The Butlers**—*the rich, white family Circe works for; they killed Macon Dead I (Jake) in order to take possession of his property.*

**Singing Bird (Sing)**—*Pilate and Macon's mother. She is a woman of mixed races, including American Indian.*

**Nephew**—*the only nephew of Reverend Cooper. He drives Milkman to visit Circe.*

**Fred Garnett**—*the driver of the Chevrolet who gives Milkman a ride in the direction of Danville after Milkman visits Circe.*

**Mr. Solomon**—*the owner of Solomon's General Store in Shalimar, Virginia. He is no relation to the immediate Solomon family.*

**Children**—*a group of youngsters who sing the song about Solomon in Shalimar, Virginia.*

**Saul**—*Shalimar resident who comes to blows with Milkman.*

**Omar**—*Shalimar resident who invites Milkman on the hunting trip.*

**King Walker**—*the gas station owner and ex-star pitcher of the black baseball leagues who helps outfit Milkman in hunting gear for the hunting trip.*

**Luther Solomon**—*a Shalimar resident who goes on the hunting trip. He is not related to Mr. Solomon.*

**Calvin Breakstone**—*Milkman's partner on the hunting trip. He tells Milkman about Ryna's Gulch.*

**Small Boy**—*a Shalimar resident who goes on the hunting trip.*

**Ryna**—*Solomon's wife; Ryna's Gulch is named after her. Legend has it that when the wind hits the ravine, it sounds like a woman crying.*

**Vernell**—*the woman who prepares breakfast after the hunting trip. She gives Milkman information about "Sing" and about Heddy Byrd.*

**Heddy Byrd**—*the mother of Sing(ing) Byrd (or Bird) Dead. She is Macon Dead II's grandmother and Milkman's great-grandmother. She is an Indian woman.*

**Susan Byrd**—*Milkman's cousin. She tells him about his family history.*

**Sweet**—*She is Milkman's lover in Shalimar. It is the first time Milkman has a loving relationship.*

**Grace Long**—*a local school teacher and a friend of Susan Byrd's. She flirts with Milkman and steals his watch.*

**Lilah**—*cousin of Susan Byrd who "passes" for white.*

**John**—*cousin of Susan Byrd who "passes" for white.*

**Crowell Byrd**—*only referred to, he is Susan Byrd's father.*

**Lilly**—*the owner of Lilly's Beauty Parlor.*

**Marcelline**—*an employee of Lilly's Beauty Parlor.*

**Shalimar**—*another name for Solomon, Milkman's great-grandfather who escaped slavery by flying back to Africa and leaving his wife Ryna and 21 children behind. The name Solomon and the title of the novel are a biblical reference to a book of the Bible in the Old Testament, also referred to as Canticles. Solomon was the King of Israel in the tenth century.*

**Old Man in House**—*the man who Milkman helps lift a crate. Guitar later tells Milkman that he is sure the crate is filled with the gold Milkman has kept for himself instead of sharing it with Guitar.*

### Summary of the Novel

This *bildungsroman*, or coming-of-age novel traces the birth, youth, and maturation of the protagonist, Milkman Dead. Born in Michigan in 1931 by miraculous means, Milkman is a gifted child until he learns at the age of four that humans cannot fly. Changed by this revelation, he grows up a spoiled, self-centered child. Torn between the magical, spiritual world of his father's sister, Pilate, and that of his greedy property-owning father Macon Dead, Milkman follows in the footsteps of his father and becomes Macon's assistant. Burdened by his parents' unspeakable confidences and troubled by his loveless household, he seeks solace at his Aunt Pilate's and by spending time with his best friend, Guitar Bains.

Living a spoiled, infantile existence until the age of 31, Milkman's sole reason for being is to seek pleasure. After a 14-year relationship with Pilate's granddaughter, Hagar, loses its lustre, Milkman decides to end it. Hagar has become too accessible, and their love-making, which so tantalized Milkman when he was younger, has lost its appeal. Distraught by Milkman's mistreatment of her, Hagar repeatedly tries to kill him.

Guitar further complicates Milkman's life when he confesses to Milkman that he is a member of a radical organization, the *Seven Days*, that avenges the unprosecuted deaths of innocent blacks by randomly killing whites under similar circumstances.

Lacking a social consciousness and fed up with the serious-ness of life, Milkman decides he needs to separate himself from his oppressive world by traveling. When Macon suggests that Milk-man steal a sack which ostensibly has gold in it from Pilate's house, Milkman sees the gold as a way to finance his trip and finally be independent.

Macon tells Milkman that the gold is from a cave near Danville, Pennsylvania, the town Macon and Pilate grew up in. Macon ex-plains that he and Pilate lived in the cave for several days after their father was murdered by a white family who wanted the Dead prop-erty. When a white man approached the cave, a fearful Macon killed him, suspecting him of being one of the men that killed Macon Dead I. Afterwards, he and Pilate discovered gold in the cave, but Pilate and Macon argued when Pilate told Macon it was morally wrong to keep it. This argument created a permanent breach in their relationship.

Macon now tells Milkman that he believes Pilate went back to the cave to retrieve the gold. Without expressing any concern for the morality of his actions, Milkman agrees to steal the gold with the help of Guitar, who wants the money to finance his vigilante organization. After stealing the sack, the two men discover there is no gold in it, only what they believe are a white man's bones. These are, ostensibly, the bones of the white man Macon killed in the cave, the bones that the ghost of Macon Dead I told Pilate to go back and retrieve because "You just can't fly on off and leave a body."

Undeterred by this first dead-end, Macon suggests that the gold must still be in the cave in Pennsylvania. Milkman agrees to go to Danville to search the cave for the gold. Milkman seeks out Circe, the midwife who delivered Macon and Pilate. Through Circe, Milkman learns the names of his paternal grandparents—Jake and Sing—and the location of the cave where Milkman believes the gold is. Milkman searches Hunter Cave and determines that the gold and the bones of his grandfather are no longer there. From what Circe tells Milkman, he concludes that the bones in Pilate's sack must be those of Pilate's father.

Less interested in his family history then in finding the gold, Milkman proceeds to Shalimar, Virginia, the birthplace of his paternal grandparents. In the all-black town, he finds the men hostile toward his urban manners and his lack of community etiquette. Milkman is perplexed by this reception after he was treated with such "southern hospitality" in Danville, where his family was the "object of hero worship."

The men of Shalimar invite Milkman on a hunting trip. On the trip, he discovers a new-found humility and an appreciation of community when he is forced to work with and rely on his fellow man. Milkman reflects on his mistreatment of his family, and of Pilate and Hagar, and develops a social consciousness. While in the woods, Guitar, who believes Milkman has hoarded the gold for himself, unsuccessfully tries to kill Milkman. Milkman protests that there is no gold, but Guitar doesn't believe him.

No longer interested in gold, Milkman resolves instead to search for his family name and history. Ultimately, Milkman realizes the final piece of the puzzle to his family name can be found in the song the Shalimar children are always singing. Overjoyed at the realization that the Solomon that the children sing of in their song is Milkman's paternal great-grandfather, he returns home to Michigan to share the information with his family.

Upon Milkman's arrival, he discovers that Hagar has killed herself. Remorseful, and taking responsibility for something for the first time in his life, Milkman takes a grieving Pilate to Shalimar to bury her father's bones at Solomon's Leap, near his birthplace.

After the burial, Guitar appears, and in the darkness accidently shoots Pilate dead. As Milkman makes out Guitar's figure on a distant rock, he leaps from the cliff he is standing on and flies into the air toward Guitar's arms.

### *Estimated Reading Time*

Since each page contains about 400 words, the average student would take approximately two minutes to read each page. The total reading time of the 341-page book would be between 11 and 12 hours. The best approach is to read the book according to the natural chapter breaks.

# Song of Solomon

## Epigraph

The purpose of an epigraph, or inscription at the beginning of a novel is to introduce the major themes of the text. The epigraph of *Song of Solomon* introduces the motifs of flying and naming as key elements to understanding the novel.

The flying motif derives from black spirituals and the gospels, and particularly from the legendary folktale of the flying African. This myth, which has been handed down from generation to generation, perpetuates the belief that black people can fly. The belief in the actual physical ability to fly is less important than the belief in flight as a metaphor for freedom, spiritual transcendence, or an escape from something unpleasant by divine means. Even after death, it is believed that the spirit flies back to the home of the ancestors of the dead person.

Milkman Dead, the protagonist of *Song of Solomon*, traces his family origins and discovers that his great-grandfather, Solomon, escaped from the oppression of slavery by magically flying away to his homeland. Reclaiming African myths of the past and, consequently, learning of his ancestral roots, are the keys to self-discovery for Milkman.

Equally important to Milkman's quest for identity is the recovery of his true name. Historically, Africans enslaved in America often lost their original names to slave names. Milkman's paternal grandfather's name was misrecorded, when he registered as a freedman in 1869, as Macon Dead. With the loss of its family name, the

Dead family is severed from its ancestral roots. It is only when Milkman journeys to Shalimar, Virginia, from his home in Michigan, that he solves the riddle of the song of Solomon and recovers his family name.

"Solomon done fly, Solomon done gone, Solomon cut across the sky, Solomon gone home," the children sing.

The song mythologizes and keeps Milkman's family history alive. With the recovery of his family name, Milkman redeems the history of his people that has been lost by an intentional erasure of African American culture at the hands of slavery.

# Chapter 1

New Characters:

**Robert Smith:** *life insurance agent and member of the Seven Days; he attempts to fly*

**Dr. Foster:** *father of Ruth Dead, and the only colored doctor in the city. "Not Doctor" street is named after him. Died in 1921*

**Ruth Dead:** *Milkman Dead's mother; Macon's wife, and the "first colored expectant mother" to give birth at Mercy Hospital*

**First Corinthians:** *Milkman's older sister by 13 years*

**Magdalene (Lena):** *Milkman's oldest sister by 14 years*

**Pilate Dead:** *Milkman's aunt and "spiritual mother." Macon's sister. The mother of Reba and grandmother of Hagar. Pilate sings the blues song about "Sugarman" in the first chapter*

**Freddy:** *one of the Dead family tenants, a janitor. He gives Milkman his nickname. Identified as the "gold-toothed man"*

**Midwife:** *character who delivers Macon Dead I's daughter, Pilate. Later identified as Circe*

**The Nurse:** *white nurse who gives orders at the scene of Robert Smith's suicidal flight*

**Mrs. Bains:** *identified as "the stout woman." Grandmother of Guitar Bains*

**Cency:** *Guitar Bains' mother and Mrs. Bains' daughter*

**Guitar Bains:** *Milkman's best friend and future member of the Seven Days. Referred to only as the "cat-eyed boy" in the first chapter*

**Macon "Milkman" Dead:** *the protagonist of the novel, and the only son of Macon and Ruth Dead; technically, he is named Macon Dead III*

**Macon Dead II:** *Milkman's father and Ruth's husband*

**Macon Dead I:** *Macon Dead II's father and Milkman's grandfather*

**Henry Porter:** *Macon Dead's tenant and member of the Seven Days. Attempts to commit suicide in the first chapter*

**Reba Dead:** *Illegitimate daughter of Pilate Dead and mother of Hagar; Milkman's first cousin*

**Hagar Dead:** *daughter of Reba, granddaughter of Pilate, and cousin of Milkman Dead*

### *Summary*

This chapter tells of the circumstances surrounding Milkman Dead's birth in 1931 in an unidentified, racially divided city in Michigan. The day before Milkman's birth, a crowd gathers on the street to watch Robert Smith jump from the hospital roof. His flying leap is accompanied by the singing of Pilate Dead.

Just as the singer predicts, a pregnant Ruth Dead experiences labor pains upon seeing Smith's suicidal flight. The next day, Ruth is the first "colored" woman to give birth at the hospital. Pilate nurtures and sings to the newborn Milkman until her brother Macon banishes her from the Dead home.

The entire Dead family lives "under the frozen heat of (their father's) glance." Ruth sustains herself by gazing at a watermark on the dining room table that marks the spot where a Waterford Bowl imported from England held flower arrangements when she was a girl. She is especially soothed by nursing Milkman, until the too-old child and mother are caught in the act by the probing eyes of Freddy.

Macon refuses to call his son by the nickname, Milkman. When upset, Macon fondles the keys to the properties he owns. The

properties give the greedy landlord his only sense of self-worth. Macon is emotionally and sexually estranged from Ruth. Although, they continue to live together in her father's house, they are extremely bitter toward each other.

Macon forbids Milkman to visit Pilate, whom Macon had cared for when he was a boy. However, at the end of the chapter, Macon wanders to Pilate's house on a whim.

Pilate, who was born without a navel and has her name inscribed inside an earring that she always wears, is singing with her family when Macon arrives in her yard. Macon is hypnotized by their voices.

### Analysis

The opening scene establishes many important themes of the novel. The flight metaphor, which begins and ends the novel, is accompanied by Pilate's blues song about flying. The singing of the song establishes a link between Sugarman and Solomon, Milkman's great-grandfather who flies home at the end of the story.

Pilate sings to Milkman when he is a child, and Macon is drawn to Pilate's singing at the end of the chapter. Singing brings people together; it is a metaphor for community and memory. Pilate's singing causes Macon to reminisce about his past, recalling the "fields, and wild turkey and calico" of his rural Southern youth.

Metaphors of singing and flying surround Milkman's birth. It is possible for Ruth Dead to be "the first colored expectant mother" to give birth at Mercy Hospital because of Robert Smith's flight. Flying is a metaphor for the impossible becoming possible. Milkman is filled with imagination and hopefulness until he learns that humans can't fly.

One of the most important conflicts in the chapter is the conflict of character-against-character. Macon is in conflict with most of the characters in *Song of Solomon*. However, his most significant opponent is Pilate. Macon, "a propertied Negro" who exploits poor blacks, is embarrassed by his sister, who he refers to as "a raggedy (wine) bootlegger." Once they had been very close, but now Macon fears her negative influence on his family. As characters, Macon symbolizes money, property or society while Pilate symbolizes myth, spiritual freedom, family roots, or nature. This creates a nature vs. society conflict. Pilate combines nature (she smells like a forest, and chews pine needles) and the miraculous (she has no navel).

Macon is symbolized by a set of keys which are a metaphor for property. Mrs. Bains says of Macon: "A nigger in business is a terrible thing to see," when Macon denies her an extension of time to pay her rent. Mrs. Bains is being critical of Macon's lack of sympathy for poor blacks. Meanwhile, Macon boasts about his showy house and car, and dresses up his family to exhibit them like expensive possessions. Macon has forgotten about his community. He has acquired the values of the most mean-spirited of white capitalists. Macon forbids Milkman to visit Pilate because Macon wants Milkman to choose his material world over Pilate's natural one.

The naming motif is prevalent throughout the first chapter. After her father is killed, Pilate has her name encased in an earring so she will never be separated from it. Macon Dead chooses the name Pilate because the illiterate man thinks the word "looks like a tree" protecting a "row of smaller trees." The tree rooted in the ground by reaching toward the sky is a symbol of the cosmos—both earth and sky united in a harmonious whole.

The Dead family, whose name has been erased by a drunken, white, Yankee soldier, has lost touch not only with its original name, but as a result, its heritage. Macon, shamed by Milkman's nickname and aware of the history of misnaming and lost names that are the legacy of slaves, thinks: "Surely...some ancestor...had a name that was real. A name given to him at birth with love and seriousness."

It is through a refusal to adopt the official names of the white community that the black community forges a history. Names such as "Not Doctor" street, and "No Mercy" hospital recall a meaning and therefore a past for the black community. Rather than using official names that have no meaning to them, the black community keeps their history alive through naming. Therefore, they can draw on these names to help recall their history in the present and in the future.

The first chapter abounds with imagery. When Ruth nurses a too-old Milkman, she envisions that "his lips were pulling from her a thread of light," (metaphor) as if she were "spinning gold." (metaphor)

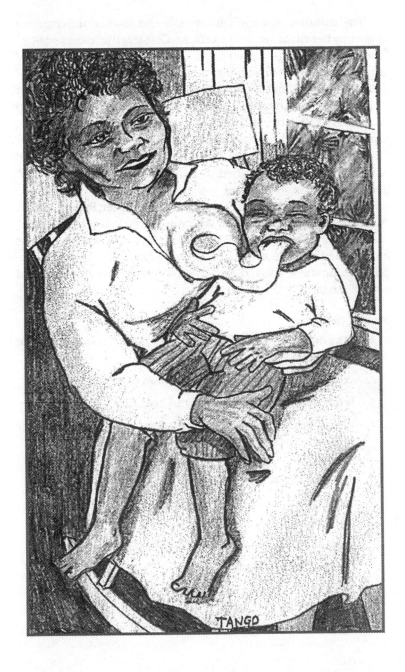

The author uses significant details and sensual descriptions to portray her characters. For example, Guitar is the "cat-eyed boy." Freddy is the "gold-toothed man." Ruth Dead is the "rose-petal lady," and Pilate Dead is the "singing woman." Pilate's "signature" descriptions also include her earring, her lack of a navel, and her "moving lips." In Chapter 1, her mouth is described as "chew(ing) pine needles," and her lips are "alive with small movements." These images will recur throughout the novel.

Hyperbole , or exaggeration for the sake of emphasis, is used when Mrs. Bains is described as being able "to move the earth" because of her imposing size.

There is much color imagery in the first chapter. Robert Smith's "wide blue silk wings" contrast with Ruth's "red velvet rose petals."

Ruth's watermark on the Dead's dining room table is used as an extended metaphor when it is described as "a mooring, a checkpoint, some stable visual object that assured (Ruth) that the world was still there...."

### Study Questions

1. Why does Mercy Hospital have an unofficial name, and what is that name?

2. What is the name of the poor section of town?

3. What does Robert Smith wear to help him fly?

4. What does the narrator say Milkman thinks of himself after he learns he can't fly?

5. Why does Dr. Foster want a centerpiece on his dining room table, and what does it signify?

6. What fairy tale does Ruth compare nursing her son to? What is the significance of it?

7. What are the two names of Macon Dead's office?

8. How is Pilate named?

9. How are pine needles significant in Pilate's life? What do they symbolize?

10. Why does Macon go to Pilate's house?

## Answers

1. Mercy Hospital is called "No Mercy" Hospital by the black residents because they are not permitted to enter the hospital.

2. The name of the poor part of town is Southside.

3. Robert Smith wears "wide blue silk wings."

4. Milkman "lost all interest in himself" when he learned he couldn't fly. "To have to live without that single gift saddened him and left his imagination so bereft that he appeared dull even to the women who did not hate his mother."

5. Dr. Foster sees the centerpiece as a symbol of wealth and refinement to distinguish his family from "the people among whom they lived." He wants to show his superiority over the lower classes.

6. Ruth compares the nursing of Milkman to the spinning of gold in Rumpelstiltskin because it gives Ruth a feeling of possessing a magical form of power.

7. The names of Macon Dead's office are "Office" and "Sonny's Shop."

8. Pilate's father chooses her name randomly from the Bible, based on the shape of the word's letters, because he is unable to read.

9. Pilate sleeps on pine needles in her mattress, and she likes to chew them. Pine needles symbolize nature.

10. Macon goes to Pilate's house because there is no music in his own home. Macon says "he wanted just a bit of music—from the person who had been his first caring for."

## Suggested Essay Topics

1. Discuss the way different characters are named. Are some names more valid than others? Why or why not?

2. Show the conflict of nature vs. society in the characters Pilate and Macon. How do their homes, possessions, and behavior reflect this conflict?

# Chapter 2

New Character:

**Mary:** *the barmaid and part-time owner of a bar in the Blood Bank, where Milkman and Guitar often go to drink*

*Summary*

Macon Dead's Sunday afternoon ritual is to show off his success by driving his well-heeled family across town to the wealthy, white neighborhoods in his expensive automobile. On these trips, Dead investigates new real estate markets. The year is 1936, and Macon contemplates the idea of an all-black vacation community in Honoré, similar to the summer resorts for white people.

A young Milkman is forced to sit backwards in the car in order to be able to see out the window. No one gets pleasure from the ride except Lena and Corinthians who pretend they're fairy princesses being driven by a prince. When Milkman has to relieve himself in the woods, Lena is elected to go with him. While relieving himself, Milkman accidently sprays Lena with urine.

The black people who see the car pass by make fun of the severe and passionless Dead family, which rides joylessly in its "hearse" without exhibiting any "real lived life" in the car.

When Milkman is 12 years old, his friend Guitar takes him to his Aunt Pilate's house for the first time. There, Milkman learns that the image of Pilate portrayed by his father is untrue; she is neither dirty nor drunk. Instead, Milkman is entranced by this remarkable woman and the sights, sounds, and smells of the mythic Pilate's world. The atmosphere and Milkman's conversations with Pilate arouse deep feelings in him. Pilate tells Milkman about his grandfather's death at the hands of white men. Milkman meets Pilate's daughter, Reba, who repeatedly wins prizes without even trying and Pilate's granddaughter Hagar, with whom he falls helplessly in love. Milkman believes that he is completely happy for the first time in his life.

When Macon finds out that Milkman has been at Pilate's, he scolds him, but he grows sentimental. Macon tells Milkman stories of his Pennsylvania childhood, farming side-by-side with his

father on the land they called "Lincoln's Heaven." Macon explains how his father, Macon Dead I, got his name from a drunken, white Yankee when he registered as a freedman in 1869. His light-skinned mother, who looked white, told Macon I to keep his new name to wipe out the past. Macon Jr. confirms Pilate's story of how their father was killed. In spite of Macon's fond remembrances of his childhood, when he carried his baby sister Pilate to another farm in his arms every morning, Macon forbids Milkman's return to Pilate's house. Instead, Macon gives Milkman a job as Macon's assistant.

### *Analysis*

Macon Dead lacks any joy in his life, even when driving his big, flashy car. The townpeople refer to it as a "hearse" because Macon Dead is characterized as "life denying." Macon Dead's Sunday trips are both a way to display his wealth and to seek new real estate markets. Embracing the worst values of white middle-class capitalism, Macon worships a "god" of money and material possessions. By capitalizing on the new black bourgeoisie and the rise of land ownership among them, Macon is exploiting his own people. Additionally, by contemplating the creation of a separate black community, Macon is indirectly sanctioning segregation. His Sunday drives, which for another family might be pleasurable family outings are, instead, "too important to enjoy."

In the traditional patriarchal or male-headed family, men, work outside the home, while the female sphere is the home, and not the world outside. While Macon functions in the public realm— the world outside is his reality—Ruth functions in the private realm.

Much evidence was given in the first chapter to reveal that Ruth is not very successful at domestic tasks. She cannot cook and she is not a traditional nurturing mother-figure. Therefore, Ruth doesn't perceive her family members as subjects, but as objects of her domestic world which she is proud to show off: she wants to display her family.

The flying motif reappears in Chapter 2, and continues to structure the novel and to be associated with Milkman. On the Sunday drives, Milkman is forced to look through the back window of the car to see, and he feels like he is "flying blind." Even as a child, Milkman is conscious of his lack of an identity: "not know-ing where he was going—just where he had been—troubled him."

Milkman's urinating on Lena, although unintentional, is a pre-monition of things to come. Urinating functions as a metaphor, indicating that Milkman will "piss on" his sisters, and all women, in the future.

Contrasted to the patriarchal household of Macon Dead is the matriarchal, or woman-headed, household of Pilate Dead. The blackberry-lipped Pilate defies female stereotypes. She is comfort-able in the domestic realm: she makes a perfect soft-boiled egg—a female fertility symbol—but unlike most women in 1943, she is self-supporting. Pilate earns her living by making wine (a symbol of youth and eternal life). Unlike Macon, however, Pilate has no interest in money or in accumulating possessions. Pilate disrupts female norms by dressing in men's shoes and being almost as tall as Milkman's father. She looks like a big, black tree (metaphor), and Milkman resolves "that what with the earring, the orange, and the angled black cloth (of her dress), nothing—not the wisdom of his father nor the caution of the world—could keep him from her."

Being associated with Pilate gives Milkman a sense of pride in his family name for the first time. Ruth may be Milkman's birth mother, but Pilate is his spiritual mother, the "pilot" who will guide him on his journey to self-discovery. The earthy, but mythic, Pilate's house is filled with a narcotic "piny-winy" smell and streaming sunlight. Her speech is organic, a stream-of-consciousness flow that doesn't proceed in the normal, linear way. She tells the time of day by citing the sun's position in the sky. Her sense of time is cy-clical. It is not the traditional, linear clock-time, it corresponds to the life cycle and seasons.

Pilate embraces both the earthy symbols of nature—her smell is the smell of fermenting fruit—and myth. Guitar and Milkman's burning question when they arrive at Pilate's house is "Do you have a navel?" In their minds, her status rises considerably with her admission that she doesn't.

Pilate defamiliarizes or shows language and color in a new and unfamiliar way. When Guitar greets her with "Hi," she says, "What kind of word is that?" She explains that each color has many varia-tions. Black can appear silky or woolly; green can be like a grasshopper or a cucumber. In this way, she challenges the preconceived notions, the "taken-for-grantedness" of daily existence.

Compared to the practical Macon who is fixed in a material reality, Pilate is an idealist who believes that reality is whatever one believes. As an example, she cites the story of the man who was standing in his kitchen but was certain he was actually falling off a cliff. Pilate, believing the man's story because it is what is real to him, offers to keep him from falling. As soon as Pilate lets go of the man, he drops to the floor dead. For Pilate, "What you believe, is what is real."

When Milkman arrives home from Pilate's house, Macon scolds him. However, Macon becomes reflective about a past he usually never recalls because Macon has no use for his origins. Macon tells Milkman about his rural Southern youth, when family mattered to him. Macon Dead I and II shared a strong father-and-son bond, working the farmland at "Lincoln's Heaven." Macon recalls the "tender, sweet, juicy" taste of turkey, his affection for the farmyard animals, fruit trees, and "the prettiest mountain" Macon ever saw (nature imagery). This perspective establishes a now-severed bond that Macon Jr. once had with nature before he lost his sense of roots, family, and his Southern values.

It is because Milkman has gone to Pilate's that Macon is flooded with memory; Pilate is a link to the past. When Macon reminisces about his father, Milkman notices the change in his tone of voice; it is "less hard" and sounds more "comfortable" and "Southern."

Family history and values are associated with the South; the North is symbolic of the corruption of these values.

Although Macon Dead I died protecting the property he loved, Macon Jr. hasn't learned the lesson of nurturing the land from his father. Instead, Macon has twisted his father's values. Macon is merely a heartless slumlord, with no regard for the land. Rather than teach Milkman the lessons of his upbringing (respect and love for the land), Macon advises his son to "own things....Then you'll own yourself and other people, too."

Macon's concept of land values is not only a result of greed it is also an act of self-protection. Money protects him against racism because he can insulate himself.

After telling Milkman the story of his father's misnaming,

Macon tells Milkman that Macon's mother's skin was light-colored: "Me and Pilate don't take nothing after her. If you ever have a doubt we from Africa, look at Pilate. She looks just like Papa and he looked like all them pictures you ever see of Africans."

Macon's identification with Africa, like his earlier identification with the South, is indicative of those things from his past which he has lost in the refashioning of himself into a petty-minded capitalist.

Men's names in the novel often describe a function, a wish, or a memory. Guitar's name describes a wish. He doesn't play guitar, but when he "was real little...(he) wanted to...."

Pilate's household abounds with much nature and color imagery:

> About Pilate:
> "Her hair was wrapped in black too, and from a distance, all they could really see beneath her face was the bright orange she was peeling." "They didn't want an egg, but they did want to be with her, to go inside the wine house with this lady who had one earring, no navel, and looked like a tall, black tree." "Her voice made Milkman think of pebbles. Little round pebbles that bumped up against each other." "Her lips moved as she played an orange seed around in her mouth. Only after the eggs were split open, revealing moist reddish yellow centers did she return to her story."

> About Reba and Pilate:
> "Her hands were stained with blackberry juice, and when she wiped her tears she streaked the purple from her nose to her cheekbone." "Mama can go for months without food. Like a lizard." "With the quickness of birds, the heads of Pilate and Reba shot up."

Macon tells Milkman a fable or allegory about a snake, using the animal as a metaphor for Pilate.

Characters continued to be described by one or two characteristics: because of his imposing size Macon Dead is described by Milkman as "Bigger even than the house they lived in." Ruth is associated with the flowers she cultivates: rhododendron, dahlias, geraniums, and imperial tulips. Corinthians and Lena Dead are described by their pale eyes and even paler skin. Corinthians' hair is "lightweight...the color of wet sand." Rather than being directly told that the girls have features that correspond to a white standard of beauty, these sparse characteristics allude to or hint at this information.

### Study Questions

1. What meaning did the Sunday afternoon rides have for Macon and Ruth?

2. Which direction does Milkman ultimately face in the car What does he see when he faces forward?

3. Why is the car called Macon Dead's hearse?

4. How does Guitar describe Pilate's house?

5. Does Milkman feel differently about his last name (Dead) after he visits Pilate? How?

6. What does Pilate say about the color black and the color green?

7. What does Pilate know about her mother's bonnet? What doesn't she know about her mother?

8. Why does Pilate say a brother and a cousin are the "same thing," even if they don't have the same mother?

9. What does Pilate think of being scared of something that isn't real?

10. Why doesn't Macon want Milkman to visit Pilate?

### Answers

1. For Macon, the Sunday afternoon drives were a way to show off his wealth and look for new real estate markets. For Ruth, the drives were a way to display her family.

2. Milkman faces backward in the car. When he faces forward, he can only see "the laps, feet, and hands of his parents, the dashboard, or the silver winged woman poised at the tip of the Packard."

3. The car is called Macon Dead's hearse because with the exception of Lena and Corinthians, the car has "no real lived life at all."

4. Guitar describes Pilate's house as "Shiny and brown. With a smell."

5. Milkman always disliked his name, but with Pilate he acts as if "having the name was a matter of deep personal pride."

6. Pilate says there are five or six kinds of black and green, like the colors of bottles, a grasshopper, a cucumber, lettuce, or "green like the sky is just before it breaks loose to storm."

7. She knows her mother's bonnet is blue like the sky, but she doesn't know her mother's name.

8. Pilate says they are the same because you have to treat them both the same.

9. Pilate believes that believing something is real is enough to make it real. Belief is reality.

10. Macon doesn't want Milkman to visit Pilate because Pilate "can't teach (Milkman) a thing (he) can use in this world."

### Suggested Essay Topics

1. Discuss "food and animal imagery" in Pilate's house. Consider the five senses, especially sight and smell, to describe the atmosphere of the household.

2. Why is Milkman drawn to Pilate's house? What do he and Guitar observe? What does Milkman say and do differently than when he is in his own house?

# Chapter 3

New Characters:

**Feather:** *he is the pool hall owner in the crime-riddled section of town called the Blood Bank*

**Railroad Tommy:** *one of two owners of Tommy's Barbershop on Tenth Street. He is a member of the Seven Days*

**Hospital Tommy:** *one of two owners of Tommy's Barbershop and a member of the Seven Days*

**Anna Djvorak:** *the Hungarian woman who credits Dr. Foster with saving her son's life in 1903. Ruth Dead comes to her granddaughter's wedding*

**Father Padrew:** *the Catholic priest who presides over Mrs. Djvorak's granddaughter's marriage, and who gives communion to Ruth Dead*

**Empire State:** *he is a Seven Days member who kills a white boy in a school yard after the historic figure Emmett Till is lynched*

**Emmett Till:** *historic figure; a 14-year-old black boy who is lynched by whites after whistling at a white woman in Mississippi in 1955*

*Summary*

Milkman continues to form an identity separate from Macon, but he is kicked out of Feather's pool hall because Macon is his father. Railroad Tommy, one of the barbershop owners, lectures Milkman and Guitar about all the things they will never have or experience because they are black men.

When Milkman is 14, he discovers that one of his legs is shorter than the other. This imperfection assures Milkman that he could never emulate his father. Because of his limp, Milkman relates to President Franklin Roosevelt, who had polio.

Chapter 3 begins in 1934 and ends in 1955. In 1943, in the midst of World War Two, Milkman is 22 years old. He has been dating Hagar and other girls for six years. Because of his relationships with the opposite sex, he sees his mother Ruth in a new light. Rather than just being the woman who cared for him, Milkman sees the smallness and limits of his mother's pathetic world.

One day, Macon and Ruth's antagonistic relationship explodes. Ruth tells a self-deprecating story which enrages Macon when she ends it by saying she is "her daddy's daughter." Milkman defends her by pulling Macon off her and threatening Macon. Milkman is both ashamed and exhilarated by his action, but not one family member shows gratitude for his good deed. Confused, Milkman reflects on his identity and his place in the world.

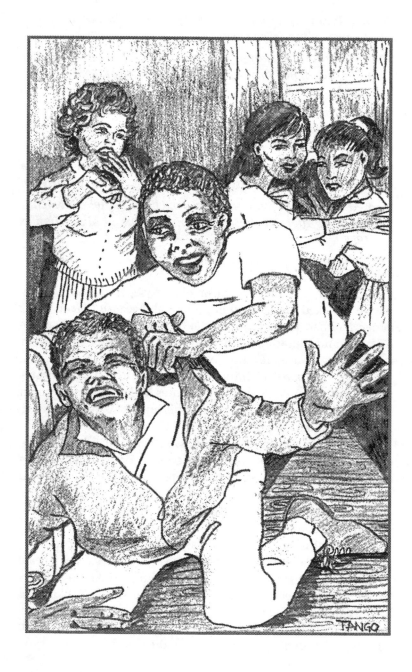

Macon explains the reasons behind his actions to Milkman. In spite of Milkman's resistance, he is forced to hear Macon's version of the history of Ruth and Macon's relationship. Macon tells Milkman that his maternal grandfather was a racist snob and that he and Ruth considered Macon a "hick" from the South. They flaunted their upper middle-class Northern upbringing in Macon's face. Macon severed all sexual relations with Ruth, when in 1921, at the time of Dr. Foster's death, Macon discovered Ruth lying naked next to the dead man with his fingers in her mouth.

Unable to bear Macon's "truths," Milkman leaves the house and searches for Guitar, to get his best friend's sympathy and "read" on everything Milkman has just been burdened with. As he walks along the street, the incestuous image of his mother lying with her own father triggers a deeply buried memory of Ruth nursing Milkman. Gradually, the vague, piecemeal memory comes more sharply into focus. Ashamed and repulsed by his recollection, Milkman questions his self-worth and the value of his life. While he is walking he puzzles over an enormous flow of people passing him in the opposite direction at a time in the evening when the streets are usually empty.

Milkman finds Guitar at Tommy's Barbershop, where a group of men are gathered, listening to a radio report about the lynching of Emmett Till in Mississippi. Guitar is incensed by the Till tragedy, but Milkman, lacking any degree of social consciousness, is indifferent to it. At the end of the chapter, Milkman tells Guitar about his defense of Ruth and the origin of his family name. Guitar tells Milkman he can empathize with him. Guitar makes an analogy between Milkman's act and Guitar's accidental killing of a doe on a hunting trip, hoping it will help elucidate why Milkman acted as he did.

### Analysis

As the chapter opens, Railroad Tommy uses the rhythmic tone of the preacher and the repetitious phrasing of poetry to lecture Milkman and Guitar about all that will be denied them because of racism. The phrase "You (are) not going to have...." takes on a musical quality as it is repeated over and over again to give the effect of a sermon. The narrator uses both repetition and cataloguing, or listing, to emphasize all the things Milkman and Guitar will be denied over the course of their lives because of their race.

Milkman, however, is having difficulty enough dealing with the present, let alone the future. The reference to Milkman's different leg lengths is referred to as a "deformity" that is "mostly in his mind." Milkman's preoccupation with his shorter leg is typical of a self-conscious adolescent, but it is also a metaphor for Milkman's low self-esteem and a moral deficiency in Milkman's character.

Milkman is gradually establishing a separate identity from his father "...he (Milkman) differed from him (Macon) as much as he dared. Macon was clean-shaven; Milkman was desperate for a mustache. Macon wore bow-ties; Milkman wore four-in-hands...."

Milkman feels "secretly connected" to President Roosevelt (FDR), in spite of the fact that President Truman "had set up a Committee on Civil Rights." (These historical allusions ground the fictitious novel in a historic reality.)

Milkman's preference for FDR emphasizes his self-interest. In spite of the fact that the people in the black community were "raving about Truman," Milkman's preferences are solely personally motivated; he has no race consciousness.

The narrator exhibits Milkman's moral deficiency and alienation from his community in two ways. First, the crowd, agitated by the murder of Till, symbolically walks in the opposite direction from Milkman. Second, when Guitar makes an analogy between Milkman and Till, Milkman says, "Yeah, well, fuck Till. I'm the one in trouble."

Since Dr. Foster's death, Ruth is emotionally bereft. Her only companions are goldfish, rhododendron, and other flowers—things that cannot hurt her as her father did when he abandoned her by dying. Ruth's only communication with Macon is based on self-humiliation. When Milkman is moved to defend his mother, Ruth, as usual, plays the role of the "honest buffoon" in order to provoke her husband. Ultimately, Macon berates her by telling her, "You make a fool of yourself."

After Macon raises his fist to Ruth, Milkman tells him, "You touch her one more time, and I'll kill you." With Milkman's bravado comes "infinite possibilities and enormous responsibilities," neither of which Milkman is mature enough to accept. At the age of 22, Milkman is still in a state of infantilism; that is, he is still a child who has not developed into a self-sufficient adult. In spite of this, no child should have to hear the illicit and intimate details of his or her parents' personal relationship.

Milkman's relationship with his sisters is not an interactive one. When he looks at their eyes after his brief "triumph" over his father, "they returned him a look of hatred so fresh, so new, it startled him." All women are synonymous to Milkman. He admits he cannot "distinguish" his sisters "(or their roles) from his mother." Like his father, Milkman sees all women as ancillary to "his privileged maleness."

Milkman's sisters have no illusion that he is defending his mother because he is acting "generous" or "wide-spirited." Milkman admits to himself that his mother is someone "whom he almost never thought about." Ruth is a non-person to Milkman, and when Milkman looks at his own reflection in his bedroom mirror, he becomes aware of his own deficiencies: his image lacks "coherence, the coming together of the features into a total self."

Macon tells Milkman that Dr. Foster—always class-conscious—despised his own people, referring to the "Negroes in town" as "cannibals," and adhering to a belief in the superiority of light-skinned "Negroes." The refined Dr. Foster's derisive treatment of the Southern "hick" who owns property in "Shacktown" incenses Macon, who feels he is made to feel worthless because of his social status.

The combination of Macon's story and Milkman's recollection of his mother's illicit nursing of him disrupts his sense of identity and shatters his emotional bond with his mother. "His mother had been portrayed not as a mother who simply adored her only son, but as an obscene child playing dirty games with whatever male was near—be it her father or her son."

Therefore, Milkman's self-worth is at its lowest ebb: "Milkman wondered if there was anyone in the world who liked him. Liked him for himself alone."

When Milkman is finally with the sympathetic Guitar, the latter tells Milkman a story about accidently killing a doe. Guitar can empathize with Milkman's distress: Defending a vulnerable woman is similar to protecting a doe. Guitar's story reveals not only his sympathetic nature, but also his strong relationship to the earth. He is a "natural born hunter," who has an instinctive bond with the land of his Southern youth, and he retains that bond.

Guitar exhibits his wisdom by telling Milkman: "People do funny things....Things that make us hurt one another....Try to understand it, but if you can't, just forget it. And keep yourself strong, man."

Upset by his nickname, and thinking about names in general—and Hagar's in particular—Milkman thinks "Pilate knows. It's in that dumb-ass box hanging from her ear. Her own name and everyone else's. Bet mine's in there too."

Consequently as the chapter concludes, Milkman continues to believe that Pilate has the answers to the questions of life, including naming.

The omniscient narration used by the author allows for a wide variety of points of view and is the appropriate narration for oral storytelling, which is the product of not one but many voices. The omniscient narration facilitates the interweaving of past and present, history and myth, fables and fairy tales, and song to create a rich tapestry of language. Dialogue is used prominently in *Song of Solomon*, allowing characters to tell their histories in their own words. Black dialect is prevalent throughout the text, and gives an authenticity to the characters.

Some visually impressive metaphors and similes in the chapter include:

> "Guitar took the opportunity offered by Feather's new target to shoot his hand out like a double-edged hatchet slamming into a tree."

> "There was quite a bit of pie filling oozing around the edge of the crust in 1945. Filling that could be his....And years later when the war was over and that pie filling had spilled over and into his very lap, land stickied his hands and weighed his stomach down into a sagging paunch, he wished he had still strangled her back in 1921." (Also a historical allusion)

Money motifs that symbolize the Foster's "black bourgeois"

values include the Waterford bowl and dining room table sent from England, Mr. Foster's two-horse carriage, and his "beautiful hands."

### Study Questions

1. Why does Milkman feel closer to President Franklin Roosevelt than to his father?

2. Why is Ruth jealous of death?

3. What does Ruth say to Macon that precipitates Macon smacking her in the jaw?

4. What word did Dr. Foster use to refer to the "Negroes" in the town? What was he most interested in when he delivered Milkman's sisters?

5. How were Lena and Corinthians' names chosen? Who else's name was chosen by this method?

6. Why does Macon tell Milkman the story about his mother?

7. Does Milkman love his mother? Why or why not?

8. What horrible secret does Macon tell Milkman?

9. What does Macon's story compel Milkman to remember?

10. What news is being broadcast over the radio when Milkman arrives at Tommy's Barber Shop?

### Answers

1. Milkman feels closer to the late FDR because FDR had polio and Milkman believes one of his legs is shorter than the other. Milkman's father is too perfect for Milkman to be like him.

2. Ruth is jealous of death because when her father died, she felt he purposely chose death because it was "a more provocative companion" than she was. Ruth felt "personal failure" and "rejection."

3. Ruth tells Macon, "I certainly am my daddy's daughter."

4. Dr. Foster called the "Negroes" in the town "cannibals," and wanted to know if Milkman's sisters' skin color was light or dark.

5.  Lena and Corinthians' names were picked randomly from the Bible. Pilate, Reba, and Hagar's names were also chosen from the Bible.

6.  Macon wants Milkman to understand his actions and to explain why he hit Macon's mother.

7.  Milkman doesn't love his mother because "she was too insubstantial, too shadowy for love."

8.  Macon tells Milkman that Ruth had some kind of sexual relationship with her father.

9.  Macon's story compels Milkman to remember that Ruth nursed Milkman when he was too old to be nursed.

10. The news broadcast at Tommy's Barber Shop is that (Emmett) Till, a young "Negro," was "stomped to death" in Mississippi for whistling at a white woman.

### Suggested Essay Topics

1.  Describe Dr. Foster. Consider the evidence and use it to indict him as a snob and a racist.

2.  Discuss the difficulties Milkman has growing up. Explains the symbolism of his "limp." Describe what he sees in the mirror, and how family "truths" skew Milkman's whole sense of identity. Discuss his relationship with the members of his family. How do these relationships impact his sense of self?

# Chapter 4

New Character:

**Winnie Ruth Judd:** *convicted murderess whom the blacks in the novel identify as an example of "white madness"*

### Summary

Despite being 31 years old when the chapter begins, Milkman continues to face an identity crisis. He is bored with life and realizes he has no real goals or ambitions. Contemplating what Christmas gifts to give Hagar, Milkman decides that he has lost interest in her after a 14-year relationship. Rather than buy Hagar a gift, Milkman decides to enclose cash in the "Dear John" letter he sends to her. In the impersonal letter he writes, he abruptly ends their relationship, thanks Hagar, and expresses his gratitude to her for the time they have shared. Hagar is enraged by the inclusion of the word "gratitude" in the letter and "the flat-out coldness" of the "thank you."

Along with the deteriorating relationship with his family and Hagar, Milkman's friendship with Guitar has begun to suffer. Milkman feels Guitar has changed considerably from the street roaming, party-seeking companion whom Milkman once knew and loved. In Milkman's opinion, Guitar has become morally superior, racially obsessive, and overly serious. The two friends often find themselves in heated arguments about class and race issues. Milkman begins to wonder about Guitar's secret life. Milkman often finds Guitar among the group of men that gather at Tommy's Barber Shop to discuss the issues of the day. Similar gatherings take place in the poolrooms and wherever men congregate in Southside.

Milkman has a disturbing dream, if it is, in fact, a dream. He dreams that his mother is being suffocated by a gardenful of overzealous plants. What is particularly bewildering about the dream is his smiling mother's benign reaction to the plants' vicious onslaught.

### Analysis

Milkman lacks both the Christmas spirit and a sense of community spirit. Having "stretched his carefree boyhood out for 31 years," Milkman reevaluates his life. He concludes that it "was pointless, aimless, and it was true that he didn't concern himself an awful lot about other people." Milkman's total lack of respect for Hagar is indicated, for instance, by his reference to her as a "honey pot" (metaphor), a mere receptacle for his male pleasure.

Milkman is a product of upper middle-class complacency. He not only lacks values, he lacks ambition and initiative because his has truly been a superfluous existence.

Guitar criticizes Milkman's utilization of his free time because Milkman spends 50 percent of his "brainpower thinking about a

piece of ass." (metonymy) Guitar tells Milkman it "looks like everybody's going in the wrong direction but you" when Milkman admits to Guitar that he continues to go "wherever the party is." Guitar's new asceticism (he doesn't want to "party," talk about girls, or get high) bothers Milkman. Milkman admits to being bored by everything. But Milkman is particularly bothered by "the racial problems that consumed Guitar" which were "the most boring of all."

In Milkman and Guitar's heated debates, they reveal various important conflicts. There is a class conflict between rich and poor. Milkman reflects the values of the Downtown, the black property-owning bourgeoisie. Guitar represents the considerations of Southside, the ghetto where incidents of racism are not averted by a "fat wallet." The men in Southside gather in the poolrooms and Tommy's Barbershop to discuss race issues. They are the chorus—the voice of the people, the social consciousness of the community. This class difference between Southside and the Downtown is reflected in the description of Christmas ornaments in the two locations. Southside has "feeble wreaths and lights" and "tacky Yuletide streamers and bells." In comparison, the rich Downtown had lights that were "large, bright, festive and full of hope."

Milkman and Guitar also represent the conflict between North and South. Milkman's all-black beach resort of Honoré, which his father owns, is symbolic of the rich North. In contrast, Montgomery, Alabama is symbolic of the South.

The year is 1963; it is the height of the Civil Rights movement. Montgomery is particularly renowned for its stand against racism, when its African American citizens, in the celebrated Montgomery Bus Boycott of 1955, refused to ride on segregated buses.

Guitar criticizes Honoré, a place where he says he will only go "with a case of dynamite and a book of matches." Milkman counters that by telling Guitar that Guitar is "mad at every Negro who ain't scrubbing floor and picking cotton." Guitar criticizes Milkman's inability to live in a place like Montgomery, Alabama, saying that Milkman is "a man that can't live there" because "if things ever got tough," Milkman would "melt."

Milkman continues to be oblivious to the struggles of African-Americans. His indifferent attitude is epitomized when he is asked indirectly what year Emmett Till is killed. Milkman responds by saying, "I don't know. I can't remember the dates of murders I haven't committed."

In the course of Milkman's discussion with Guitar, he tells Guitar of a dream he had about his mother. The plants in Ruth's garden "surround" and "smother" her. But instead of being scared, Ruth smiles as they take away her breath "with their soft jagged lips." This use of personification, or giving non-human things human qualities, reveals the clandestine or secret life of Ruth. Her interaction with the living things in her garden is symbolic of a profound act of communion with the earth associated with female fertility. Milkman, because he is male, is unable to comprehend this life-affirming female act of creation.

The image of Pilate's mouth continues to identify her. When her peace and well-being are disrupted, her lips are still. When Reba is attacked by a physically abusive boyfriend, (Pilate's) lips "didn't start moving again until he was out of sight and running down the road."

Another recurring image is the facial features of women reflecting a white standard of beauty. When Hagar jealously observes Milkman's new girlfriend's "gray eyes," it is the impetus that triggers Hagar's desire to kill Milkman. "The gray eyes," and "silky copper-colored hair" of the girl reflect a white standard of beauty that the dark, African-looking Hagar is unable to compete with.

The author also uses fairy tale allusions prominently in the text. Here is how Hagar is described in the chapter: "The calculated violence of a shark (metaphor) grew in her, and like every witch (simile) that ever rode a broom straight through the night to a ceremonial infanticide as thrilled by the black wind as by the rod between her legs; like every fed-up-to-the-teeth bride (simile) who worried about the consistency of the grits she threw at her husband as well as the potency of the lye she had stirred into them; and like every queen and every courtesan (simile) who was struck by the beauty of her emerald ring as she tipped its poison into the old red wine, Hagar was energized by the details of her mission.

### Study Questions

1. What are some of the metaphors Milkman uses to describe Hagar?

2. What one gift that Hagar receives is especially out of place in her house?

3. What book does Pilate read?

4. What happens to Pilate's mouth when she is upset?

5. Why does Reba want to be a patient in a hospital?

6. Does Guitar like Honoré? What does he call it?

7. What does Milkman equate being serious with?

8. What are some of the violent flower images the narrator uses to describe the garden in Milkman's dream?

9. Who does Freddy say killed his mother?

10. Who else besides Guitar does Freddy say should know about the "strange things" going on in town?

### Answers

1. Milkman refers to Hagar as "his private honey pot" and "the third beer."

2. The one gift Hagar receives that is especially out of place in her household is a bathrobe, because she has no bathroom.

3. Pilate reads a fourth-grade geography book.

4. When Pilate is upset, her mobile mouth becomes still.

5. Reba wants to go to the hospital because she thinks it's a "nice hotel."

6. Guitar doesn't like Honoré. He refers to it as a "nigger heaven."

7. Milkman equates being serious with being "miserable."

8. Some of the violent flower images the narrator uses to describe Ruth's garden are the "bloody red heads," and "the bobbing snapping heads" of the flowers with "their soft jagged lips."

9. Freddy says that ghosts killed his mother.

10. Freddy tells Milkman that besides Guitar, he should ask Corinthians about the "strange things" going on in town.

### Suggested Essay Topics

1. Discuss why Milkman is no longer interested in Hagar. Explain what attracted him to her in the first place and what has changed. Why does Hagar's accessibility make her less attractive?

2. List the different crimes mentioned in the chapter. Determine if all of them are real or if some are fictitious. What is the impact of interweaving history with fiction?

# Chapter 5

New Characters:

**Moon:** *character who aids Guitar in preventing Hagar from killing Milkman*

**Preacher:** *head of family who took in an orphaned Pilate at age 12 when Pilate decided to search for her extended family*

**Pickers:** *migrants who Pilate lived and worked with for three years when she lived in New York State. They evicted her from their midst when they found out she had no navel*

**Father of Reba:** *Pilate's lover on the Virginia island where she gave birth to Reba*

### Summary

In this chapter, Milkman conceals himself in Guitar's room in order to avoid a spurned Hagar, who is intent on killing Milkman. Guitar continues to criticize Milkman's selfishness, his lack of a social consciousness, and his Northern ways, (ways Guitar equates with white middle-class materialism.) But regardless of Milkman and Guitar's striking differences, they continue to care about each other.

In spite of their closeness, each of the friends knows the other has a secret. Guitar is afraid because Milkman is indifferent toward the prospect of death, and Guitar fears for Milkman's life, but Guitar doesn't know what is at the source of Milkman's indifference. Milkman has his suspicions about Guitar's covert activities and is on the verge of discovering that Guitar is a member of the Seven Days.

One early morning Milkman confronts his mother after he's followed her out to the cemetery where her father is buried. He learns his mother's version of Macon's story. Ruth tells Milkman that Macon is responsible for her father's death and that he also tried to kill Milkman before he was born. Ruth tells Milkman about his parents' estranged relationship. She denies an incestuous relationship with her father. She tells Milkman the details surrounding his birth: Pilate's magic concoction enticed Macon to impregnate Ruth. When Macon found out about the pregnancy, he attempted to abort Milkman. Pilate intervened, and gave Ruth a protective girdle to guarantee Milkman's unobstructed birth.

Ruth admits to nursing Milkman, but she tells him she also prayed for him. "What harm did I do you on my knees?" she asks him, and the question unceasingly repeats itself in Milkman's mind.

The burden of this additional family information makes Milkman feel "like a garbage pail for the actions and hatred of other people." As a result, Milkman finds himself attracted to the prospect of death because "afterward there would be no remembrance of who he was or where." Hagar breaks into Guitar's room and manages to stab Milkman in the shoulder.

When Ruth discovers Hagar's intention to kill Milkman, she goes to Pilate's house to confront Hagar. But Pilate intervenes, telling both women Milkman "wouldn't give a pile of swan shit for either one of you." A discussion about death ensues, and Pilate tells Ruth that she still communicates with her dead father. Pilate tells Ruth the history of her life. After separating from Macon, Pilate travels for 20 years. She lives with a preacher's family, with "pickers" or migrants, and with an island clan in Virginia where she gives birth to Reba. After her daughter's birth, her father's ghost appears to Pilate. He tells her to "Sing," and adds that "You just can't fly off and leave a body." Responding to his words, Pilate believes she

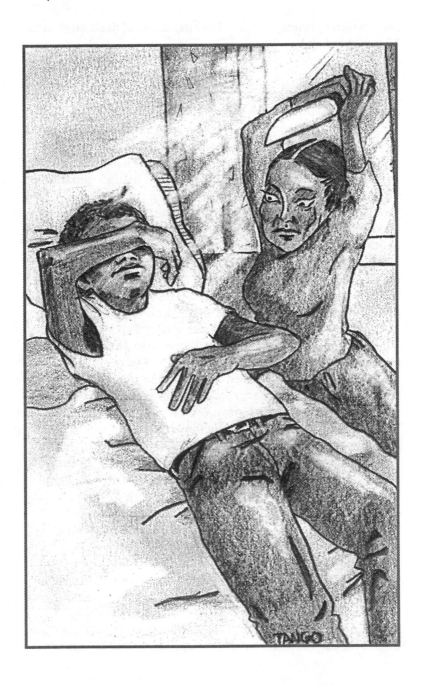

must return to Pennsylvania to bury the bones of the man she and Macon murdered.

### Analysis

Chapter 5 continues to compare and contrast Milkman and Guitar's characters. They are divided along class lines—Milkman is rich; Guitar is poor. They disagree on race issues: Milkman is indifferent or "bored" with race issues; Guitar is developing a "black power" mentality, similar to Malcolm X and the Nation of Islam with its radical solutions to racism and belief in black separatism. They are vehement about their distaste for the other's preferred geographic locale: Milkman stereotypes the South as an unenlightened, poor, and backward community; Guitar stereotypes the North as an immoral, racist version of Babylon.

In this chapter, when Guitar challenges Milkman's beliefs, rather than attack him in his usual humorless, serious manner, Guitar uses what appears to be "jive-talk" or bantering to get his points across to Milkman. Guitar's playful, clever dialogue is highly ironic, i.e., its meaning is the opposite of what Guitar actually says. For example, Guitar tells Milkman, "I live in the North now. So the first question comes to mind is North of what? Why, north of South. So North exists because South does. But does that mean North is different than South? No way! South is just south of North...."

In another example of irony, Guitar says to Milkman, "Black? White? Don't tell me you're one of those racial Negroes? Who said anything about black people. This is just a geography lesson."

As the chapter progresses, Milkman's sense of self continues to deteriorate. Family history in the form of oral history (or history by word-of-mouth) is an important way in many cultures, including African American culture, that the past is transmitted from generation to generation. Unfortunately for Milkman his immediate family history is not only unbearably painful, it also exposes him to conflicting versions of this history and he cannot determine which version is true. This history tells Milkman nothing about the values of his African American heritage. Milkman "wanted to escape what he knew, escape the implications of what he had been told."

Chapter 5 contrasts not only Milkman and Guitar, it also portrays Ruth and Pilate in a character-against-character conflict.

Ruth grew up in "a great big house" but was "pressed...into a small package," first by her father and then by her husband. Ruth is a symbol of the white plantation owner's genteel wife, commonly referred to in literary criticism as "the ideal Southern white lady." In spite of her Northern upper middle-class upbringing, she is representative of the oppressed Southern white woman of history. This woman's function is to be a well-dressed mannequin, a decoration for the household, a pretty possession. Even as a child, Ruth is treated as a pretty object. She has no friends, she says, "only school-mates who wanted to touch my dresses and my white silk stockings."

In contrast, Pilate does not live in a "great big house." Until she comes to Michigan, she lives, briefly, in a cave, on an island, and out in nature. Unlike Ruth, who has stayed in one place her entire life, Pilate travels extensively for 20 years and the landscape is her university.

While Ruth sees herself as Milkman's "home," it is not a home where the heart is. It is more like a museum that houses a "beautiful toy." Milkman is a symbol, and Ruth perceives his death "as the annihilation of the last occasion she had been made love to." Her desire for physical pleasure is displaced onto her son.

The narrator incorporates a list of opposites to contrast Ruth and Pilate. Ruth is described as "lemon-skinned." Pilate is described as black as night. Ruth is "corseted." Pilate is "buck naked" underneath her dress. Ruth is well-read and ill-traveled. Pilate reads only a fourth grade geography book, but she collects a rock from every state she's been to. Ruth needs money and exquisite possessions to live. Pilate is indifferent to both money and things. But in spite of their differences, the women share a ground of common understanding because of their concern for Milkman and their bonds with their dead fathers.

Pilate tells the story of her past, and her oral history helps to piece together the puzzle of the Dead family's past. When Pilate tells her story, she reveals that she was "cut off from people early." She "birthed" herself, and was discriminated against because she lacked a navel. People, being characteristically fearful of what is different, ostracized Pilate. When Pilate realized that all women didn't lack navels, she asked "What's it for?" "It's for...it's for people

who were born natural," she was told. So, Pilate lived from place to place, on the fringes of society. She never committed herself to a community or a man for any substantial length of time because it was inevitable that her lack of a navel would be discovered. This resulted in her extreme isolation, but this isolation gave her an opportunity to become independent, and to think for herself.

Ultimately, Pilate rejected the way the "civilized" world lived, and constructed her own values based upon what made her happy, what she needed "to know to stay alive," and "what is true in the world." Armed with an instinctively caring and moral nature, Pilate "acquired a deep concern for and about human relationships."

Pilate is a natural healer and conjure woman. Evidence of her mythological stature includes the fact that she "birthed" herself, that she has no navel, and that she cast a spell over Macon to conjure him to desire Ruth. Then Pilate put a juju doll with "a round red circle painted on its belly" in Macon's office and gave Ruth a protective girdle to safeguard Milkman's birth.

Pilate exhibits the wisdom of a sage and the fortune-telling powers of a seer: "Ain't nothin' goin to kill him (Milkman) but his own ignorance, and won't no woman ever kill him. What's likelier is that it'll be a woman save his life."

This chapter contains many figures of speech; the following are a few examples:

"Fear lay like a pair of crossed paws on his chest." (simile)

"Ain't nobody giving up no head." (pun)

"My name is Macon. I'm already Dead." (pun)

Hagar's obsessive love of Milkman is described by Ruth:

"She had no self left. She (Ruth) was not looking at a person but an impulse, a cell, a red corpuscle that neither knows nor understands why it is driven to spend its whole life in one pursuit: swimming up a dark tunnel toward the muscle of a heart or an eye's nerve end that it both nourished and fed from." (metaphors)

Pilate's mouth continues to be characterized; in this chapter it is described as "busy lips."

### Study Questions

1. Do Guitar and Milkman get along better or worse after their quarrel about Honoré versus Alabama? Why?

2. Why does Guitar say Southerners can relate to Jesus?

3. Why does Guitar tell Milkman that a "Negro" can't be an egg?

4. How often does Hagar attempt to kill Milkman?

5. Where does Milkman follow Ruth to?

6. What words does Ruth use to describe her father's moral character?

7. Who aided Ruth in saving Milkman when Macon tried to abort him?

8. When was the last time Ruth and Macon had physical relations before they conceived Milkman? How many years elapsed between then and when Milkman was conceived?

9. What did Pilate give Ruth to entice Macon into sleeping with her?

10. What piece of fruit does Pilate offer Ruth both times that she visits? Why can't Ruth eat it?

### Answers

1. Guitar and Milkman get along better after their quarrel because of its cleansing effect on their relationship: "They were easy with each other now that they didn't have to pretend."

2. Guitar says Southerners can relate to Jesus because they can relate to his being "strung up on a tree."

3. Guitar says a "Negro" can't be an egg because his genes won't allow it: "Nature says no."

4. Hagar attempts to kill Milkman at least once every month.

5. Milkman follows Ruth to the Fairfield Cemetery where her father is buried.

6. Ruth describes her father's moral character by saying he "was not a good man," and that he was "arrogant," "foolish," and "destructive."

7. Pilate aided Ruth in the preservation of Milkman's life.

8. The last time Ruth and Macon had physical relations was before Dr. Foster died. Therefore, they didn't have relations for ten years.

9. Pilate gives Ruth "some greenish-gray grassy-looking stuff" that has to be mixed with rain water, and then put in Macon's food in order to entice Macon to sleep with her.

10. Pilate offers Ruth a peach both times she visits, but Ruth can't eat peaches because the fuzz tickles her nose.

### Suggested Essay Topics

1. Discuss the things in Ruth's cloistered world that makes her life bearable. Why do these things comfort Ruth?

2. Discuss Pilate's association with magic in the chapter. Cite all the magical aids she uses to achieve her ends. Is her magic always benevolent magic?

# Chapter 6

### Summary

Guitar tries to make Milkman take responsibility for Hagar's anguished state of being after Milkman has severed their relationship. Milkman objects to Guitar's constant criticism of him and Guitar's new conservative ways. Guitar no longer wants to party or have fun. Guitar finally reveals the reason behind his behavior. He tells Milkman about his membership in the Seven Days society, formed in 1920. The organization has its own code of justice because the white laws and courts don't protect the black community. In the event that an innocent black is victimized, and the criminal is not brought to justice, the Days seek retribution. An innocent white will be killed on the same day of the week as the black person. Each of the seven members has been assigned a day of the week, and the randomly selected victim must be killed in a similar way to the method of death experienced by the black. Guitar's assigned day is Sunday. When Milkman objects to the Days' killing of people, citing its lack of morality, Guitar tells him, "We're not killing people," we're "killing white people." Guitar does not see the killings as an act against humanity. He sees it as an abstraction, a mathematical equation in order "to keep the ratio (of whites to blacks) the same." "There's too much wrong with it," Milkman says, and compares Guitar to Malcolm X.

### Analysis

Milkman is unable to accept responsibility for his mistreatment of Hagar. Ever since he was initiated into sex, he has used women to sexually gratify himself and has never thought of them as anything but sex objects.

In Guitar's racist view, he categorically identifies all whites as unnatural, as "an evil force." While Milkman lacks a social consciousness, he can still recognize that what Guitar is doing is abominable and morally wrong. When Guitar says "There are no innocent white people," that every one of them "is a potential nigger-killer," he is making a judgment solely on skin color. "The disease they have is in their blood, in the structure of their chromosomes," he tells Milkman.

Milkman says, "I can't see how it (the retributive killing) helps anybody." Guitar talks about abstractions instead of the concrete act of murdering human beings. Guitar rationalizes his actions by citing the black man's poverty, how he has no money and no court of his own to affect the balance of things. Milkman, who has never lacked money is, not as sympathetic to this as Guitar. Milkman is afraid of Guitar's lack of morality, and tells Guitar, "if you do it enough, you can do it to anybody."

Milkman suggests Guitar change his name to Guitar X, after Malcolm X, to replace his slave name. But Guitar shows no interest in replacing his slave name. He tells Milkman that "Guitar is my name. Bains is the slave master's name and "I'm all of that." His name is part of his history. The name Bains contributes to his rage, and his rage allows him to act without conscience.

### Study Questions

1. According to Milkman, what vices has Guitar given up?

TANGO

2. What does Guitar say about white people as a race? Does he believe all white people have the potential to kill?

3. Does Milkman "buy into" Guitar's views of white people? Why or why not?

4. What does Guitar say about the Mafia and the Klan?

5. What historic names does Guitar cite as potential killers?

6. Why did Robert Smith commit suicide and why did Henry Porter try to?

7. What does Guitar mean when he says of Robert Smith, "we do that rather than crack and tell somebody?"

8. Can Guitar have a family life as a member of the Seven Days?

9. What does Guitar say when Milkman says that there's "no love in it," referring to the Seven Days?

10. Why does Milkman "take Guitar to task" when Guitar says "we don't off Negroes"?

### Answers

1. According to Milkman, Guitar has given up "smoking," "fucking," and "drinking."

2. Guitar says that as a race, white people are "unnatural." He believes because they're "unnatural" that any one of them has the potential to kill.

3. No, Milkman does not agree with Guitar. He thinks Guitar is unfairly stereotyping white people.

4. Guitar says the Mafia "kills for money," and the Klan "kills for fun."

5. Guitar cites the names of John F. Kennedy, Albert Schweitzer, and Eleanor Roosevelt as historic figures who would kill black people if the opportunity arose.

6. Robert Smith and Henry Porter tried to commit suicide because they were Seven Days' members, and the responsibility got to be too much for them.

7.  When referring to Robert Smith, Guitar means that Seven Days' members would take their own lives before betraying their cause.

8.  No, as a member of the Seven Days , Guitar cannot marry or have children.

9.  Guitar tells Milkman that the Seven Days is about love. Guitar says, "It's about loving us. About loving you. My whole life is love."

10. Milkman criticizes Guitar when Guitar says, "We don't off Negroes" because Milkman has said to him, "You can off me." Rather than think of Milkman as an individual, Guitar categorizes him first by what race Milkman is.

### Suggested Essay Topics

1.  Discuss Guitar's criticism of white people. Why do you think his views are so extreme? Does the novel or your own experience suggest that any of his views are justified? Give reasons why or why not.

2.  Discuss Milkman's condemnation of Guitar's organization, the Seven Days. What important points does Milkman make? Is he able to influence Guitar's thinking? What additional arguments could Milkman have brought up to oppose Guitar's views?

# Chapter 7

### Summary

Chapter 7 continues the theme of Milkman's search for self. Milkman concludes that he needs distance from his family, and "bit" by the "wandering bug," he makes plans to leave. Macon tries to detain him, telling Milkman "Money is freedom."

When Milkman lets slip that Pilate has a green sack in her house with her "inheritance" in it, Macon concludes its the long-lost gold that he and Pilate discovered in a cave after their father died when Macon was 16 years old. Macon relays the story of how he and Pilate were homeless after their father was killed. Macon buried his father in a shallow grave, and Circe, the midwife, took them into her white slavemaster's house, where she hid them.

Children of nature, Macon and Pilate suffered greatly, cooped up in a room, eating "the soft, bland food" of white people. While there, Pilate had her father's hand-written piece of paper with her name written on it put into her mother's brass snuff box. A blacksmith fashioned it into the earring Pilate always wears.

Fearful of being discovered, the children return to nature and ultimately are led to a cave by the ghost of their father. While in the cave, Macon kills a threatening-looking white man, and they discover gold. Pilate forbids Macon from taking the gold because it is morally wrong. But "life, safety, and luxury fanned out before (Macon) like the tailspread of a peacock." The once loving brother and sister suffer a rift over the gold. Macon continues to hold a grudge into the present. He tells Milkman the gold must be in the green sack in Pilate's house. The "snake" has been in possession of the gold the whole time! Macon tells Milkman if he steals the gold from Pilate, Macon will give him half of it.

### Analysis

The circumstances surrounding Milkman's birth and his desire for travel recalls the mythological journey of the classical hero in Greek and other literature. The mythological hero experiences a miraculous birth, is initiated into manhood, separates from his family by taking a long journey, and then returns to share his newfound knowledge and take his place in the community.

Paramount in importance to this chapter is the lengths to which the Dead men will go for the sake of money without concerning themselves with the moral consequences. Macon is willing to direct his son to steal from his own sister. "Money is...the only real freedom there is," he tells Milkman.

In the chapter, Milkman complains that he feels "used" by everyone, as they make him "the subject of their dreams of wealth, of love, or martyrdom." But Milkman is a user, too. He uses Hagar and "throws her away"; he uses the place or sanctuary that is Pilate's home, the only place he has ever really felt complete, as the scene of thievery and betrayal. Milkman repays Pilate's love with

disloyalty and indifference. And his own father puts Milkman up to it.

Once Macon appreciated the land; the earth taught him how to live. He wanted to coexist with it, not own it. When Macon is with Pilate after their father's death both children couldn't bear being shut off from nature. Pilate cried for "her own cherries, from her own cherry tree." "At night they slept in a haystack, so grateful for open air even the field mice and the ticks were welcome bedmates." They knew the land "intimately," and Macon's instinct was to lead them to Virginia, "where Macon believed they had people." The "born-wild" Pilate and the 16-year-old Macon, who had worked on a farm since he was young, defined themselves and their values by their relationship with Nature.

When the ghost of Macon Dead I, their father, appears both of them are able to see him because they both are in sync with the cosmos. Later in life, only Pilate will be able to see her father; Macon will lose his gift of "sight."

The following example of nature imagery appears in this chapter:

> "The sun was blazing down, the air was sweet, but every leaf that the wind lifted, every rustle of a pheasant hen in a clump of ryegrass, sent needles of fear through their veins. The cardinals, the gray squirrels, the garden snakes, the butterflies, the ground hogs and rabbits—all the affectionate things that had peopled their lives ever since they were born became ominous signs of a presence that was searching for them, following them. Even the river's babbling sounded like the call of a liquid throat waiting, just waiting for them."

### *Study Questions*

1. What does Macon tell Milkman that freedom is?

2. Why doesn't Macon know that Pilate has a green sack hanging from her ceiling?

3. Where do Pilate and Macon go after their father is killed?

4. Who buries Macon's father, and where?

5. Why did the "slavemaster's" house where Circe hid the children repulse Pilate and Macon?

6. What two possessions did Pilate have that belonged to her mother? What possession of her father's did she have?

7. What happened to Pilate's ear after she put on her earring? What did Circe do to help her?

8. Where were Macon and Pilate originally headed once they left Circe's house? Why?

9. What happened to Pilate and Macon on the third day after they left Circe's house?

10. What remained in the cave and what was gone when Macon returned to it after his rift with Pilate?

### Answers

1. Macon tells Milkman that "money is freedom."

2. Macon doesn't know Pilate has a green sack hanging from her ceiling because Macon has never been in his sister's house.

3. After their father's death, Macon and Pilate are hidden by the midwife Circe at the house where she is employed. When they leave there, they live out in nature and then in a cave.

4. Macon buried his father near a stream where he and Macon Dead I used to fish together.

5. The "slavemaster's" house repulsed Macon and Pilate because they couldn't stand the stillness; they were bored cooped up in a room and shut off from nature and the sky. They couldn't eat the "soft bland food" that white people ate.

6. Pilate had her mother's brass snuffbox and sunbonnet, and the brown scrap of paper that her father had written her birth name on.

7. Pilate's ear became infected, and Circe put cobwebs on it to heal it.

8. Once they left Circe's house, Macon and Pilate were headed to Virginia because Macon believed they had family there.

9. On the third day after they left Circe's house, Macon and Pilate awakened to find the ghost of their father sitting near them.

10. When Macon returned to the cave after his rift with Pilate, the dead man was still in the cave, but the tarpaulin and the gold were gone.

### Suggested Essay Topics

1. Discuss the role of nature in Macon and Pilate's lives as children. Refer to specific descriptions of nature in the chapter. Show how nature is perceived as benevolent and as sinister by the children. Explain the discrepancy.

2. Discuss how Macon changes in the presence of the gold. Give specific examples.

# Chapter 8

### Summary

Guitar needs money for explosives to avenge the death of "four little colored girls" who have been "blown out of a church." Milkman offers Guitar one-third of the gold, if Guitar will help Milkman steal it. While discussing a plan of action, Guitar is ruthless in his conversation with Milkman. Guitar says he will "knock off" Milkman's relatives if it's necessary. "What you doin' with a heart anyway?" he asks Milkman.

Meanwhile, Milkman is preoccupied with the thought that Guitar may have already murdered for his vigilante organization. In spite of Milkman's moral opposition to the Seven Days, he is mesmerized by the prospect of murder as something "exotic." Milkman wonders how it must feel; he wonders how it would change a person. He is impressed "with the seriousness and the dread of the work of the Days," the fear they must inspire.

Milkman is giddy with the romance of him and Guitar "taking risks" again like when they were young "swashbucklers." Milkman

associates the stealing of the gold with the "old times" when they "swaggered, haunched, leaned, straddled, ran all over town trying to pick fights or at least scare somebody...." As they discuss the theft, they see a peacock weighted down by the "jewelry" of its plumage. The image triggers talk of what they will buy with the gold once they collect it. As they approach Pilate's house on the night of the theft, Milkman and Guitar are immune to the sweet smell of the night air. They can only inhale the smell of money. Pilate observes the two men entering her house and is unable to fathom why they'd want a green sack filled with a dead man's bones.

### Analysis

Milkman's sense of self continues to be unstable. While he desperately wants the mobility attaining the gold can give him, he finds it hard to make decisions not only about the gold but in life. To act, in general, is difficult for Milkman. He admits that he is unable to lead anything but a frivolous, lighthearted life because he is overburdened with his family's secrets. However, he is always quick to distribute blame to someone else for his condition.

When Guitar tells him "You got a life? Live it!" he jars Milkman into believing if he steals the gold, his self-worth will rise. Guitar's words make Milkman's *Jack in the Beanstalk* fantasy "into an act, an important, real and daring thing to do." (fairy tale allusion)

Milkman envisions himself after stealing the gold as "a self that could join the chorus at Railroad Tommy's with more than laughter." Milkman still believes that the way a man impresses another man is to show he can rule people by fear. Sharing this act with Guitar, Milkman believes, will also allow him to regain the irresponsibility and carefree feeling he experienced when he and Guitar used to terrorize the neighborhood when Milkman was 12 years old.

But Guitar has irrevocably changed from the street-roaming youngster, and subsequently, the free-thinking, caring adult he used to be. He not only makes judgments based solely on skin color, but he is gender-biased, as well. He thinks he can outfox and outslug Pilate, Reba, and Hagar because they are women. He also shows no regard for Milkman's hesitancy to want to cause bodily harm to his relatives when the two men attempt to take the gold from Pilate's house.

Two symbols stand out in Chapter 8. The pure white peacock is a metaphor for both material possessions and "emotional baggage." While the theme of flight continues to structure the text, it is always flight of an unsuccessful nature. When Milkman shows "unrestrained joy" at the precarious flight of the peacock, Guitar tells him that the bird has "too much tail. All that jewelry weighs it down. Like vanity. Can't nobody fly with all that shit. Wanna fly, you got to give up the shit that weighs you down." Guitar may give Milkman this advice, but he doesn't seem to know that there are other forms of vanity besides material possessions, the baggage of vengeance, for example, that can weigh a body down.

The second symbol is a sensory impression: the "sweetish smell" of "crystalized ginger" as it drifts to the shore on the air. The presence of this smell in the industrialized city with its polluted lake and air which kills "the hair of willows," and the "carp" in the lake sets up a conflict between society and nature. Again the theme of the corruptive force of industrialization and modernization is opposed to the regenerative and primeval healing properties of the ancestral past.

Those who have been corrupted by the comforts of modernization, such as air conditioning, are unable to smell the sweet ginger. The residents of Southside, however, who have screens or nothing covering their windows, have access to the "heavy spicy-sweet smell" of the East, the smell of the marketplace of Accra (the capital of Ghana in West Africa) with its images of "striped tents and the sha-sha-sha of leg bracelets" (onomatopoeia). Those residents of Southside who inhale deeply smell the spicy scent of memory, of hope and possibility, while Milkman and Guitar, when they smell the night-air think of "freedom...or justice, or luxury or vengeance."

When Milkman and Guitar are on the verge of cutting down the green sack from Pilate's ceiling, Guitar genuflects before a sack of fool's gold as "the figure of a man" (Pilate's father) looks disapprovingly on. The ghost here functions as a symbol both of moral conscience and of spiritual unrest.

In a lyrical passage, filled with sensual descriptions, the author uses the technique of cataloguing to portray vivid images of the pieces of cloth remaining from the dresses of the little murdered girls: "Every night now, Guitar sees little scraps of Sunday dresses—white and purple, powder blue, pink and white, lace and voile, velvet and silk, cotton and satin, eyelet and grosgrain." The narrator compares these to "the heart-red pieces of velvet" of the artificial roses petals Ruth Dead spilled from her basket in the first chapter, but unlike the rose petals the scraps of the dresses "...did not fly; they hung in the air quietly, like the whole notes in the last measure of an Easter hymn." (simile)

Again, as in the case of Emmett Till, the author makes historical allusions to events in the Civil Rights movement that impacted African American history. The date when Milkman and Guitar break into Pilate's house, September 19, 1963, is four days after the murder of the "little colored girls" who were killed during a church service at the 16th Street Baptist Church in Birmingham, Alabama.

### Study Questions

1. Why does the narrator say Milkman includes Guitar in the plan to steal the gold?

2. Why does Milkman suddenly start buying newspapers? What kind of reports is Milkman looking for?

3. As Milkman and Guitar discuss their plan for stealing the gold, what image does Milkman see as he stares "off into the sky for inspiration"?

4. Why is Milkman aware of a falseness in his voice when he talks to Guitar about what he will buy with the gold? Why does he really want the gold?

5. What does Milkman say about the way Pilate's household tells time?

6. Where does Milkman tell Guitar are the only places Pilate, Reba, and Hagar go together?

7. What smell fills the air on September 19, 1963?

8. How is the lake described at the beginning of the chapter?

9. What does the green sack hanging from Pilate's ceiling "promise"?

10. What does Guitar see in the moonlight as he and Milkman leave Pilate's house?

### Answers

1. Milkman includes Guitar in his plan to recover the gold because "maybe he wanted to see Guitar warm and joking again, his face open and smiling instead of with the grim reaper look." Milkman also wants Guitar involved because "he could look forward to both fun and fear."

2. Milkman buys the newspaper to look for "reports of murders that appeared suspicious, pointless" to determine if they are committed by the Seven Days.

3. As Milkman stares "into the sky for inspiration" he sees a white peacock.

4. Milkman notices a falseness in his voice because he is not really interested in buying things with the gold because he's always had money. He wants the money in order to be independent from his family and in order to seek new adventures: "New people. New places."

5. Milkman says that Pilate and her family are "not clock people" and that he doesn't think Pilate knows "how to tell time except by the sun."

6. Milkman tells Guitar that the only two places the Pilate household goes to together are funerals and circuses.

7. The smell of ginger fills the air on September 19, 1963.

8. The lake is described as "full of mill refuse and the chemical wastes of a plastics manufacturer."

9. The sack hanging from Pilate's ceiling "promised everything: the Risen Son and the heart's lone desire. Complete power, total freedom, and perfect justice."

10. As Guitar and Milkman leave Pilate's house, Guitar sees "the figure of a man."

*Suggested Essay Topics*

1. Compare and contrast Guitar's and Milkman's attitudes as they discuss stealing the gold. How are their words, thoughts, and actions different? Why does Guitar say Milkman is "defeatist" about the gold? Why does Milkman call it "common sense"?

2. Discuss why milkman's adolescent adventures, when he and Guitar "terrorized" the neighborhood and instilled fear in everyone, remain so important to Milkman. Give examples of some of their adventures and their symbolic meaning for Milkman.

# Chapter 9

New Characters:

**Michael-Mary Graham:** *the hack-poetess who hires Corinthians to work as a maid in her house*

**Mr. Solomon:** *the name Pilate gives to her imaginary husband, whose bones, she tells the police, are in the green sack that Milkman and Guitar steal from her house*

**Nero:** *member of the Seven Days that Milkman sees in Porter's Oldsmobile*

*Summary*

At the age of 42, Corinthians gets her first job outside the house, as a maid to an affected, hack-poetess. In spite of Corinthians refined upper middle-class upbringing and her college education, she had led a dead-end life with no prospects for marrying. Refusing to be resigned to a home-life of making artificial roses, Corinthians finally acquires her own money and independence through her new job, but she lies to her family about her work.

On the bus to work, she meets Henry Porter, a yardman who is a member of the Seven Days, and a man who isn't her social equal. While Corinthians is ashamed of him, she comes to love him anyway. When Henry finally makes Corinthians choose between being

a "doll baby" (like her mother) or being a "woman," Corinthians chooses the latter. After spending the night with Henry, her "vanity" is transformed into "self-esteem."

After Milkman and Guitar are picked up by the police for stealing a sack of human bones, Pilate plays the role of "Aunt Jemima" to get the two men out of jail. Pilate tells the police the bones in the green sack belong to Mr. Solomon, her husband. She tells the police, she had been too poor to bury the bones. Guitar, sickened by Pilate's groveling and incensed that there is no gold, looks at Pilate "with jeweled hatred in his eyes."

At home in his bathtub, Milkman reexperiences the shame of having been arrested and handcuffed. He feels remorse for his betrayal of Pilate, the woman who has loved and nurtured him throughout his life. As Milkman reflects on his disgraceful actions, he notices his legs are both the same length.

Milkman has a conversation with Lena in which his sister accuses him of having "peed" on everyone his entire life. Lena ascribes his behavior to "that hog's gut that hangs down between your legs." Lena is infuriated that Milkman betrayed Corinthians by telling Macon that Henry Porter was her lover. Lena denounces Milkman for being "exactly like (their father)."

### Analysis

The highly ironic portrayal of Corinthians and the poetess who has hired her as a maid has many humorous touches and is replete with examples of an appearance vs. reality conflict. Corinthians may be a maid, but she euphemistically refers to herself as an "amaneuensis," a "rickety Latin word" that meets with the approval of her mother and gives the appearance of a job that is "intricate, demanding, and totally in keeping with her education."

Corinthians keeps up social appearances by dressing in high heels, and only dons the necessary pair of loafers and dress once she arrives at the home of her employer.

Corinthians, like her mother, has all the qualities of the ideal Southern white woman. She is light in skin color, and has no real skills. She is a delicate-appearing ornament. She is "enlightened in education" so that she is "able to contribute to the civilization" or "civilizing of her (backward) community." In this ironic tone, the narrator equates a liberal arts education at what she considers to be an uppity rich white woman's college (Bryn Mawr) to an act of futility where one develops no useful skills to function in the practical world.

Corinthian's employer, Michael-Mary Graham, is a parody of a poet. She is characterized by all the worst stereotypes of a creative person: she can't do domestic work because of the "heavy demand of artistic responsibility." She selects "colors and furnishings" for their "inspirational value." Michael-Mary Graham speaks and thinks in clichés: concerned with hiring a frail-figured woman such as Corinthians as a maid, Michael-Mary hires her anyway because of the poetic ring to Corinthians' name.

In keeping with the theme of hackneyed poetry, the "ill-dressed" and socially inferior Henry Porter gives Corinthians a trite, clichéd poem in a greeting card to introduce himself to her. Corinthians is ashamed to be seen with Henry as the result of a class conflict. Henry is a social inferior who "doesn't even own a pair of dress shoes." In Corinthians' eyes, Henry's outward appearance takes priority over his inner being. Corinthians explains to Henry that her father "never wanted us to mix with...people." She leaves out the word "inferior," or lower-class. When Corinthians tells Henry she doesn't know when she can tell her father about him, she finds herself gesturing in the fake manner of the affected Michael-Mary. Her "fake gesture" goes along with her "fake feelings of moral and filial commitment."

Henry's patience wears thin, and he demands that Corinthians stops behaving like a "doll baby" and behave like a "grown-up woman." The 44-year-old virgin thinks to herself that she doesn't know any "grown-up women." All her role models are "doll babies," not women, but ladies, who have ultra-refined manners, but lack much else. They know a lot about appearance, but they know little or nothing about passion or reality.

Pilate, too, plays a part when she attempts to get Milkman and Guitar out of jail. She does an "Aunt Jemima" imitation, compromising herself by playing the role of a "black mammy," a stereotypical black character in white Southern literature. Pilate intentionally gives the appearance of being slow-witted and ex-

tremely yielding to accomplish her goal of having Milkman and
Guitar released from jail. After Milkman is freed, Pilate, who appeared shorter when she was playing the role of "Aunt Jemima,"
again looms tall with her head wrapped in her glorious silk rag.

Flooded by the shame of his jailing experience and his betrayal
of Pilate, Milkman tries to wash the shame off in the bathtub. He
recalls how Pilate "had brought him into this world when only a
miracle could have, and yet he showed her no gratitude." With this
admission, his legs appear to be the same length as he stares at
them in the bathtub.

Pilate, who acted as an emissary between Milkman and nature, cooked him "his first perfect egg" and showed him the sky
"so that from then on when he looked at it, it had no distance, no
remoteness, but was intimate, familiar, like a room that he lived
in, a place he belonged."

While Milkman reminisces about his fragile connection with
nature, Lena's only connection with Nature is being severed. Her
maple tree, a symbol of tolerance and endurance, is dying. The
maple tree's presence allowed Lena to ignore what was "really
wrong" in her life, including Milkman's dismissive and inhumane
treatment of her, Corinthians, and their mother." Losing the natural (the maple tree) and condemned to a life of creating the unnatural in the form of artificial rose petals, Lena vows she will no
longer make the fake petals. With that declaration, Lena also announces that she will no longer tolerate being "peed" on by
Milkman. Lena attributes Milkman's narcissism to his "hog's
gut...between (his) legs," a symbol for Milkman's single-minded
pursuit of sexual gratification at the expense of all that is human.
Lena, like Corinthians and Ruth, has spent her whole life impris-
oned in the Dead household, serving the needs of men.

She relates a story to Milkman of how when she was young,
she and Corinthians were dressed in their best clothes. Macon
paraded them in front of a group of poor and dirty children so that
the children could "see us, envy us, envy him." But Lena gives no-
tice that she will no longer tolerate being an object manipulated
by the men in her family. "I don't make roses anymore and you
have pissed your last in this house," Lena tells Milkman, to end
Part I of *Song of Solomon*.

Although the names, First Corinthians and Magdalene, called Lena, have biblical associations, the tradition of randomly choosing them from the Bible and then subverting their meaning is particularly important in the case of Milkman's sisters. The name Corinthians derives from Corinth, the ancient Greek city infamous for its luxury and debauchery. Magdalene is the name of the reformed prostitute in the New Testament, who Jesus cured of evil spirits. Both the name Corinthians and Magdalene are associated with harlotry and licentious behavior. In *Song of Solomon* names are ironic: the Dead sisters spend much of their adult lives as passionless virgins who live the most chaste and austere of existences. Therefore, their names decry traditional symbolic meanings and form a new and separate history. The "red velvet rose petals" the sisters make symbolize artificiality and the unnaturalness of the Dead women's lives.

While Ruth was associated with rhododendron, dahlias, geraniums, and imperial tulips earlier in the text, Lena too, was attracted to flowers as a child (Chapter 2) when she picked purple violet and wild jonquil. Sadly, these are both women's only real associations with authentic life. Ruth also has her goldfish and Lena had her maple tree to nurture. Without it, Lena is disconnected from life.

Guitar's "gold-eyes" or "cat-eyes" are now described by Macon as "yellow-eyed," a color often associated with cowardliness or betrayal.

### Study Questions

1. Why does Corinthians' mother approve of the title "amanuensis"?

2. What is the actual work Corinthians does?

3. What work had Corinthians done up until this point?

4. Why don't the men of the community want to marry Corinthians?

5. What college did Corinthians attend? What colleges would the men have preferred?

6. According to the narrator what did a "four-year dose of liberal education" do to Corinthians?

7.  What kind of shoes did Corinthians wear to and from work?

8.  How does Henry Porter introduce himself to Corinthians?

9.  What covers Henry Porter's walls? What do the dates signify?

10. What kind of imitation does Pilate do to get Milkman and Guitar released from jail?

### Answers

1.  Corinthians' mother approves of the word "amanuensis" because "it was straight out of the 19th century" and "the rickety Latin word" makes Corinthians' work seem important.

2.  Corinthians' actual work is as a maid.

3.  Up until this point, Corinthians had made red velvet roses.

4.  The men of the town didn't want to marry Corinthians because she "lacked drive." They believe women like her are too "accustomed to middle-class life" and that they have "no ambition, no hunger, no hustle in them."

5.  Corinthians attended Bryn Mawr. The men would have preferred that she attend black colleges such as Fisk, Howard, Talledega, and Tougaloo.

6.  A "four-year dose of liberal education" guaranteed that Corinthians "had no real skill's" and that she was "unfit for 80% of the useful work of the world."

7.  Corinthians wore high-heeled shoes to and from work.

8.  Henry Porter introduces himself to Corinthians by giving her a greeting card with a poem in it.

9.  Henry Porter has calendars covering his walls. The dates signify the days when the Seven Days are to commit retaliatory murders.

10. Pilate does an "Aunt Jemima" imitation to get Milkman and Guitar out of jail.

***Suggested Essay Topics***

1. Discuss the narrator's opinion of a "liberal education." Consider the advantages to this type of education and make an argument in its favor. Then contrast these to the disadvantages. Explain the differences between different types of education. For example, compare a liberal arts' education to a vocational education or to the type of "real-life" experience education Pilate has had.

2. Consider the conflict between appearance and reality in the character Corinthians. Describe it by her physical appearance and her actions. Does Corinthians ultimately make a choice between appearance and reality? What are her reasons for her choice and how does this choice change her life?

# **Chapter 10**

New Characters:

**Reverend Cooper:** *the Reverend of Danville, Pennsylvania who Milkman goes to visit to learn about his family's past. Milkman finds out information about where the cave Pilate and Macon lived in is located from the Reverend*

**Esther Cooper:** *Reverend Cooper's wife*

**The Butlers:** *the rich white family Circe works for. They killed Macon Dead I (Jake) in order to take possession of his property*

**Singing Bird (Sing):** *Pilate and Macon's mother. She is a woman of mixed races, including American Indian*

**Nephew:** *the nephew of Reverend Cooper. He is called Nephew because he is the Reverend's only nephew. He drives Milkman to visit Circe*

**Jake:** *the original first name of Macon Dead I*

**Fred Garnett:** *driver of the 1954 Chevrolet who gives Milkman a ride toward Danville. Garnett is insulted when Milkman tries to pay him for the Coke and the ride that Garnett gives him*

**Old man in station house:** *the man who Milkman helps lift a crate. Guitar later tells Milkman that he is sure the crate is filled with the gold Milkman has kept for himself instead of sharing it with Guitar*

## *Summary*

Relieved to leave behind "Lena's anger," "Ruth's stepped up surveillance" and Macon's "bottomless greed," Milkman begins his journey to Danville. Enthralled by an exhilarating airplane ride to Pittsburgh, Milkman "felt free...away from real life" where "the wings of all those other people's nightmares (had) flapped in his face and constrained him."

Before his journey, Milkman and Guitar continue to debate race issues, and Guitar lectures Milkman on how "Everybody wants the life of a black man."

On his journey, Milkman finds that the scenery his father raved about, because of its beauty, is repetitive and boring.

Milkman stands out in the "tiny farming town" of Danville in his "beige three-piece suit," "beautiful Florsheim shoes," and gold Longines watch. He is surprised by the community's friendliness and Reverend Cooper's affection for Milkman because Reverend Cooper "knows his people." Milkman is impressed by "southern hospitality."

His family history is more palpable to him now that he is physically in the place where it transpired. Milkman is amazed at the townpeople's high regard for his paternal grandfather and, especially, for his father. He does not recognize Macon as the spirited country boy the Danville clan loved, but he is proud and moved by the stories.

Milkman decides to go look at the Dead family farm and instead ends up at the Butlers' mansion. Milkman is surprised to find Circe alive. The ancient lady lives among a pack of dogs that have, to Circe's pleasure, destroyed the mansion. Circe hopes only that someone will find her body at her death and bury her before the dogs eat her remains. Although Circe's appearance reminds Milkman of the fairy tale witches in his nightmares, he tolerates her embrace. From Circe, Milkman learns the names of his paternal grandfather and his paternal grandmother (Jake and Sing) and the location of the cave where he believes the gold is buried.

In spite of Milkman's exposure to a wealth of family information, his top priority is still the recovery of the gold in Hunters Cave. On his trek to the cave, Milkman battles the woods, creeks, and slopes of the outdoors. He begins to appreciate the difficulty and complexity of nature, not because of any sympathy with or understanding of nature, but only as an obstacle that obstructs him from reaching his goal.

When Milkman finds the cave empty, he lets out an anguished cry, and limping from the cave, he vows to continue his journey to Virginia where he concludes Pilate must have taken the gold.

### Analysis

The text continues to be structured by the flight motif which for Milkman "encourages illusion and a feeling of invulnerability." Milkman continues to equate flight with power, but power achieved not through knowledge but through escapism. As Milkman sits in the "glistening bird, it was not possible to believe he had ever made a mistake, or could." Flight is still a fantasy to Milkman, not something he believes it is possible to attain in "real life."

Part I of *Song of Solomon* portrays the emotionally immature Milkman Dead's growing-up years, but it does not show his transformation into a self-sufficient man with a secure sense of self. Part II, beginning with Chapter 10, follows the pattern of the epic poem, as Milkman embarks on his journey to self discovery.

Traditionally in epic poetry, the hero must wean himself from his mother (separation) and depart on a journey of initiation (a test in which he acquires some new-found knowledge of himself, usually through a heroic act). Finally, the hero, who has entered the realm of manhood, is ready to return to his home, able to put his knowledge to use (Campbell, *The Hero With a Thousand Faces*, 35). Milkman will follow a similar journey.

Before Milkman leaves Michigan, his race debate with Guitar continues to surface. When Guitar is highly critical of both the "colored" and white woman's demands on the black man, Milkman asks Guitar why he is defending the "colored" woman. "Because she's mine," Guitar says. "Can't I love what I criticize?" But Milkman

**Chapter 10**                                                          83

doesn't believe its about "loving Negroes" at all, especially if you can't tell the difference between the black and white woman "except for skin color." Appearance (skin color) conflicts with reality (in the form of the inner person). "Everyone wants the life of a black man," Guitar tells Milkman. Only black men don't want to kill the black man. When Milkman gives his father as an example of a black man who tried to kill a black man (Milkman as a baby), Guitar dismisses it because Macon acts "white." Guitar also considers it an egregious sin that Pilate "slipped into those Jemima shoes" when talking to the police. He considers her behavior a form of prostituting one's self in front of white people.

While Milkman is in the South, he begins to comprehend the racial injustices his people experience. When Reverend Cooper discusses Macon Dead I's murder, Milkman asks if there was a trial to bring the white men to justice. "Arrested for what? Killing a nigger? Where did you say you were from?" Reverend Cooper asks the naive Northerner. Milkman actually feels anger for the first time and wonders why "he hadn't felt angry when he first heard about (his grandfather's death)." But when Milkman continues to pursue the gold, he admits to himself that he doesn't want it to seek vengeance on the acts perpetrated against his family. He wants the gold on its own merit in order that Milkman may "own it" and be "free." Milkman has begun to be conscious of acting for reasons other than selfish ones; however, he cannot sustain these "fine" feelings. Milkman is still motivated by a concept of how he should act, rather than acting from genuine feeling.

The theme of nature is prevalent throughout Chapter 10. Milkman continues to be oblivious to both its beauty and its power, and especially its relevancy to his life. All the living things in nature, like a human being, have a life cycle of birth, life, and death. Milkman does not accept nature the way he accepted Pilate's gift to him of the sky, as either a place of refuge or something to learn from.

When Milkman hears about the farm, "Lincoln's Heaven," growing peaches, the feasts after hunting, and "the backbreaking work of a going farm," he feels that he "missed something in his life." While in Danville, Milkman realizes that when Macon spoke of working side-by-side with his father on the farm, Macon wasn't talking about "manliness," but love of family, and of man's coexistence with the land he nurtures.

The men of Danville understand the community's connection to the land when they reminisce about the beauty and abundance of "Lincoln's Farm." Macon Dead I also makes them realize they, too, can take advantage of what the world has to offer them if an illiterate slave who lost his name can succeed. But success involves a reverence for the land, farming as a creative act, and an act of sharing: "We got a home in this rock, don't you see!…Grab it. Grab this land! Take it, hold it, my brothers, make it, my brothers…kiss it.own it, build it, multiply it, and pass it on—can you hear me? Pass it on!"

Unlike Macon Dead Jr.'s view of the land as something to use to exploit and own your own people, the working of the land in Danville is accompanied by a deeply shared communal feeling among men. Up to this point, though, Milkman sees nature as something that knocks his hat off with its branches, that has creeks "too shallow to walk" and "too rocky to swim." Milkman has "no idea that simply walking through trees, bushes, or untrammeled grass could be so hard." Rather than seeing nature as an entity that can teach Milkman about life, he still perceives of it as a powerful combatant who obstructs his path and must be conquered.

The mythic Circe appears in the text as a message-bearer who sees through Milkman's "fine feelings," telling him "You don't listen to people. Your ear is in your head, but it's not connected to your brain." Unlike the beautiful enchantress of Greek mythology, Circe is described as a wizened, wrinkled old woman with skin of "pleats and crochet work" who conjures up the image of an ancient and decrepit witch. But in spite of her physical appearance, she is timeless "with the strong, mellifluous voice of a 20-year-old." Her presence is accompanied by "the sweet spicy perfume" of ginger which connects her with Africa and the values and memories of the past. The sage-like Circe is the messenger of the oral history of Milkman's people. She "birthed" everyone in Montour County, hid Macon and Pilate after their father was killed, and gives Milkman answers to many of his questions. She is the conjure woman who, using age-old folk methods, heals Pilate's infected ear with cobwebs. Like Pilate, Circe is a larger-than-life figure who combines the earthy with the mythological in a perfect union.

With her pack of "golden-eyed dogs" and with a vengeance worthy of the gods, Circe is behind the imminent demise of the "last room" of the Butler house, the house where the last Butler, Elizabeth, "killed herself rather than do the work I'd been doing all my life," Circe says. Circe, then, is one of the carriers of the oral tradition, bringing her message of the past into the present, so that Milkman will be able to apply it to the future.

The author continues to invert the meaning of names significant in the Western canon of literature, rendering their history as meaningless. The naming of the midwife as Circe is another example of this.

A vivid portrayal of Circe is drawn: She has "dry, bony hands like steel springs" (simile) that rub Milkman's back, and a "floppy mouth" that "babbles" into Milkman's vest. The author uses physical description sparingly, but with a sharp eye for detail which creates vivid, unforgettable images.

The chapter abounds with personification, metaphors, and similes:

"He was oblivious to the universe of wood life that did live there in layers of ivy grown so thick he could have sunk his arm in it up to the elbow. Life that crawled, life that slunk and crept and never closed its eyes. Life that buried and scurried, and life so still it was indistinguishable from the ivy stems on which it lay. Birth, life, and death—each took place on the hidden side of a leaf. From where he stood, the house looked as if it had been eaten by a galloping disease, the sores of which were dark and fluid." (personification)

"A farm that covered their lives like a paintbrush and spoke to them like a sermon." (simile)

"He glittered in the light of their adoration and grew fierce with pride." (metaphor)

"As soon as he put his foot on the first stone, he smelled money, although it was not a smell at all. It was like candy and sex and soft twinkling lights. Like piano music with a few strings in the background." (similes) "He'd noticed it before when he waited under the pines near Pilate's house; more when the moon lit up the green sack that hung like a kept promise (simile) from her ceiling; and most when he tumbled lightly to the floor, sack in hand. Las Vegas and buried treasure; numbers dealers and Wells Fargo wagons; race track pay windows and spewing oil wells; craps, flushes, and sweepstakes tickets. Auctions, bank vaults, and heroin deals." (all metaphors, cataloguing)

"The crunch is here. The big crunch. Don't let those Kennedys fool you." (historical allusion)

### Study Questions

1. Why does Milkman tell Guitar he intends to go to Danville on his own?

2. What does Guitar answer when Milkman tells him "Everybody wants something from me..."?

3. What does Guitar tell Milkman about his father?

4. What does Guitar see in the eyes of his mother after the "white man" gives her $40?

5. When Guitar says "just recently one of us was put out on the street," who is he referring to? Who is the "us" in the phrase? Who is responsible?

6. What are some of the things that indicate Milkman is wealthy when he goes to Danville?

7. When Milkman meets Reverend Cooper, why does the Reverend become extremely friendly and solicitous with Milkman?

8. What does Reverend Cooper offer Milkman to drink? What is it stored in?

9. Who made Pilate's earring for her?

10. How do the men of Danville describe Milkman's father as a youth?

## Answers

1. Milkman tells Guitar he needs to go to Danville by himself because he wants to be independent and that it would look "suspicious" if two men were "roaming around the woods" looking for gold.

2. Guitar tells Milkman "They want your life, man."

3. Guitar thinks Milkman's father is "a very strange Negro" who "behaves like...and thinks like a white man."

4. "A willingness to love" was shining in the eyes of Guitar's mother when she took the $40 from the "white man."

5. When Guitar talks "about one of us being put out in the streets" he's referring to Henry Porter. The "us" refers to the Seven Days Society. Milkman is indirectly responsible for Henry's eviction because he told his father about Henry's relationship with Corinthians.

6. When Milkman goes to Danville, he has two bottles of Cutty Sark in his suitcase, and he is dressed in a three-piece beige suit, expensive shoes, and a gold watch.

7. Reverend Cooper becomes extremely friendly with Milkman because after Milkman tells the Reverend his name, the Reverend realizes that "I know your people!"

8. Reverend Cooper offers Milkman pure rye whiskey stored in a large mayonnaise jar.

9. Reverend Cooper's father, a blacksmith, made Pilate's earring for her.

10. Milkman's father is described by the men of Danville as being as "strong as an ox." He "could ride bareback and barefoot." He "outran, outplowed, outshot, outpicked and outrode" everybody.

### Suggested Essay Topics

1. Discuss images of aging and decay in Chapter 10. Cite examples of both plant life, human life, and inanimate life in your essay. Discuss the relationship between the three forms of life.

2. Discuss why the death of Macon Dead I was "the beginning of (the Danville men's) own dying." What did he symbolize for the men? What were his accomplishments? How did these accomplishments affect his moral nature?

# Chapter 11

New Characters:

**Mr. Solomon:** *the owner of Solomon's General Store in Shalimar, Virginia. He is no relation to the immediate Solomon family or Pilate's imaginary husband, Mr. Solomon*

**Children:** *a group of youngsters in Shalimar, Virginia who play a game and sing the song about Solomon that reveals the Dead family's origins*

**Saul:** *Shalimar resident who comes to blows with Milkman*

**Omar:** *Shalimar resident who invites Milkman on the hunting trip*

**King Walker:** *the gas station owner and ex-star pitcher of the black baseball leagues who helps outfit Milkman in hunting gear for the hunting trip*

**Luther Solomon:** *a Shalimar resident who goes on the hunting trip. He is not related to Mr. Solomon*

**Calvin Breakstone:** *Milkman's partner on the hunting trip. He tells Milkman about Ryna's Gulch*

**Small Boy:** *a Shalimar resident who goes on the hunting trip*

**Ryna (Ryna's Gulch):** *Solomon's wife; Ryna's Gulch is named after her. Legend has it that when the wind hits the ravine, it sounds like a woman crying*

**Vernell:** *the woman who prepares breakfast for the men after the hunting trip. She gives Milkman information about Sing and about Heddy Byrd*

**Heddy Byrd:** *an American Indian; She is the mother of Sing(ing) Byrd (or Bird) Dead. She is Macon Dead II's grandmother and Milkman's great-grandmother*

**Susan Byrd:** *Milkman's cousin. She is an American Indian who tells Milkman about his family history*

**Sweet:** *she is Milkman's lover in Shalimar. It is the first time Milkman has a loving and reciprocal relationship*

### Summary

Milkman arrives in the all-black town of Shalimar, Virginia. He is surprised by the small-town atmosphere, the customs of the people, and the facial features of the women, which resemble African features rather than those of black women in the North.

The children sing a song "about Jay...son of Solomon" and play a game that reminds Milkman of his alienation from other children as a youth because of his clothes (he was forced to wear a "velvet suit" to school) and his wealth.

Stopping at Solomon's store, Milkman is told that someone is looking for him. The man is driving a car with Michigan license plates and leaves a message which exact words should be "Your Day has come." Milkman thinks Guitar must be in trouble.

Milkman is the recipient of hostility from the townspeople. He is unaware that his behavior is superior, condescending, and inhumane. He treats the women of the town like sex objects, there merely for his pleasure. He flashes his wealth in a town where many of the men are unemployed, and therefore resentful of Milkman who treats them like "anonymous, faceless laborers." He doesn't even ask their names or introduce himself to them. Milkman perceives himself as "the object of hero worship" in Danville, and is perplexed by his cool reception in Shalimar.

After getting in a fight with the younger men of the town, Milkman accepts an invitation to accompany the older men on a hunting trip. He boasts of his hunting prowess, although he has never handled a gun before. He accepts the invitation as a dare, but also because "he had stopped evading things, sliding through, over, and around difficulties."

During the hunt, Milkman gets left behind. Alone in nature, he is disoriented by the sounds, distances, and the code of behavior he is supposed to follow: "...here, where all a man had was what he was born with, or had learned to use...." Milkman hears the

sobbing sound the wind makes as it blows through Ryna's Gulch. Alone in the darkness, he reassesses his actions and the impression he makes on others. Milkman begins to take responsibility for his behavior. Stripped down in the woods without his possessions, without "his money, his car, his father's reputation, his suit, or his shoes," to buffer him from reality, he is forced to commune with his "true" self. While out in the woods, Milkman realizes that there is another way to communicate besides through language; something more basic than language. He listens to the hunters in the distance answering to the rhythms of the animals, each other, and the earth.

Guitar makes an unsuccessful attempt on Milkman's life. Guitar is startled and runs off when Milkman shoots into the trees to scare him. Milkman's soul-searching has made him come to understand Guitar, and the world that has somehow "maimed" him.

At the conclusion of the hunting trip, Milkman admits his fear to the other hunters, something he would not have been able to do before the hunt. Humbled by the experience, Milkman experiences a strong bond with both nature and the Shalimar community. Because the men of the community have now accepted Milkman, they offer the woman Sweet to him. For the first time, Milkman makes love with a woman, not as a selfish act to fulfill his own needs, but as an act of sharing between two giving and caring partners.

### *Analysis*

The image of the strutting "black rooster" among the "white hens" and the images of the bobcat's heart and of the roots of the gum tree "cradling (Milkman) like the rough but maternal hands of a grandfather" represent the two extremes Milkman experiences in Chapter 11. The first image is a symbol of machismo accentuating male bravado. Milkman wants to impress the men by being more "macho" than they are. Consequently, Milkman grandstands and makes threatening remarks to show he can be as tough as the Shalimar men. At the beginning of the chapter, Milkman's sense of self is still predicated upon what he considers the most desirable male characteristics, those based on power and intimidation. These coveted traits include physical courage in the form of aggressive action, the ability to rule by fear, virility and sexual bragging, and arrogance.

Milkman's combines this machismo veneer with a garish display of wealth in his talk about cars, his elegant clothing, and dismissive manner. This display of wealth and disregard for the Shalimar men give the men the impression that Milkman has "the heart of the white man." That is, Milkman has lost all sense of connection with or interest in communicating with men like himself.

He treats the men of Shalimar as "laborers," because they do not matter to him as human beings. They are only commodities, useful to achieve a means to an end for Milkman. Milkman is not interested in them; he is only interested in what he can get from them, be it, a ride somewhere, shelter, food or drink, information, etc. Milkman also treats their women as commodities that can be used and discarded, the way Milkman discarded Hagar.

No one in Shalimar cares about Milkman's northern pedigree or his family name that stands for "dread and grudging respect" in Michigan.

When Milkman accompanies the older men on the hunting trip, he is not interested in learning about them and their world. He accepts the trip as a dare and a challenge to his manhood. It is only after he isn't able to keep up with the older men in the hunt that he realizes how little he knows about this world. Only then is Milkman able to admit to himself that he was involved in both the fight and the hunt as a result of ignorance and vanity on his part.

The image of the maternal grandfather cradling Milkman in his hands is a symbol of the transformed Milkman. "The sweet gum's surface roots" are personified as "the rough but maternal hands of a grandfather," accentuating a union between man and nature. With this union of man and nature comes knowledge, the sixth sense, "the one that life itself might depend on."

Once Milkman relinquishes his tired refrain that "he didn't deserve some bad luck or bad treatment from others," and instead, takes responsibility for himself and his acts, he is able to look outward away from himself and consider the feelings of others.

Milkman learns that, alone in nature and stripped of his possessions, "all a man had was what he was born with, or had learned to use. And Endurance." Milkman realizes that this lesson of nature, translates to life, too. Whether Milkman is in the Blue Ridge Country of Virginia or in an industrial city in Michigan, the essence of a man is the same; he is what he knows, and nature is the best teacher. Nature is personified and asks man to honor "her" by honoring each other and, in this way, man honors the preciousness of life itself.

The hunting trip is an initiation rite for Milkman. Once he acknowledges nature's place in his life, "he found himself exhilarated by just walking the earth, he became one with it—and ceases to limp."

By accepting the embrace of both nature and his grandfather, Milkman develops a long-absent social consciousness and a moral integrity that allows Milkman to no longer limp.

When Milkman is given the opportunity to remove the heart from the slain bobcat's body, the heart not only symbolizes Milkman's acceptance into the Shalimar fraternity, but it is also a metaphor for Milkman finally possessing a loving and good human heart.

One of the oldest male rituals of acceptance is offering a woman of the community to a man outside the community. It is a sexist act, but an ages-old male act of belonging. When Milkman unites with Sweet, the two try to outdo each other in the kindnesses they perform for each other, not because of some competition, but out of a genuine caring for the well-being of the other.

The women of Shalimar are described at the beginning of the chapter as having faces with "wide sleepy eyes that tilted up at the corners, high cheekbones, full lips blacker than their skin, berry-stained, and long, long necks." Their features are similar to Pilate's, who Reverend Cooper referred to as "pretty" in Chapter 10. However, by northern standards Pilate is criticized as "ugly." The standard of beauty in Shalimar differs from the ideal Northern view of beauty. African features are considered desirable features in Shalimar, rather than the white standard of beauty coveted by many "black" women in the North.

Folk etymology explains the confusion with the name Solomon, which variously becomes Shalimar (the natives' name of the town) and Charlemagne (the mapmakers' name for the settlement.) The pronunciation of the natives—"Shalleemone"—blends the various words being used.

Example of figures of speech used in this chapter include:

"All those shrieks, those rapid tumbling barks, the long sustained yells, the tuba sounds, the drumbeat sounds, the low liquid howm howm, the reedy whistles, the thin eeeee's of a cornet, the unh unh unh bass chords. It was all language." (onomatopoeia, musical metaphors)

### Study Questions

1. What do the Shalimar women carry in their hands? What does Milkman expect to see them carrying?

2. Why does Milkman end up buying a car to travel to Shalimar?

3. What does Milkman say about "southern hospitality"?

4. How does Mr. Solomon pronounce Shalimar?

5. What message does Guitar leave with Mr. Solomon for Milkman? What does it mean?

6. Why didn't Milkman play as a child the way the children of Shalimar do?

7. How did Milkman and Guitar originally meet?

8. What are the two major things Milkman does wrong to incite the men of Shalimar?

9. What is the name of the place where the wind sounds like a sobbing woman?

10. What does the earth tell Milkman when he listens to it?

### Answers

1. The Shalimar women carry nothing in their hands where Milkman would expect to see a pocketbook, change purse, wallet, keys, paper bag, comb or handkerchief.

2. Milkman buys a car to travel to Shalimar because the town is so small that he can't get there directly by train or bus.

3. Milkman says that southern hospitality is "for real." He wonders why "black people ever left the south," and he thinks

"the Negroes are as pleasant, wide-spirited, and self-contained as could be."

4. Mr. Solomon pronounces the name Shalimar as "Shalleemone."

5. The message Guitar leaves with Mr. Solomon for Milkman is "Your Day has come." It means Guitar is going to kill Milkman.

6. Milkman didn't play as a child the way the Shalimar children do. He was excluded from their games because he was dressed in a "velvet suit," and because of his wealth, which isolated him.

7. Milkman and Guitar first met when Guitar pulled four boys off Milkman after Milkman's nose had been bloodied in a fight.

8. Milkman talks about the Shalimar women as if they are sex objects and he announces to the men that he may have to "buy another car to get back home." He doesn't introduce himself or ask their names. He refers to the Shalimar men as "them" in their presence.

9. The place that sounds like a woman sobbing when the wind hits it is Ryna's Gulch.

10. The earth tells Milkman that Guitar is standing behind him. This realization gives Milkman enough time to "catch the wire" that Guitar is about to fasten around his throat.

### Suggested Essay Topics

1. Discuss why Milkman offends the men of Shalimar. List all the things that Milkman does to alienate the men. Compare and contrast Milkman's Northern behavior to the acceptable behavior expected in the South.

2. Discuss Milkman's uneasiness with nature. Give examples of the difficulties Milkman has while hunting and how this gradually changes. Discuss the relationship between Milkman's search for self and his understanding of nature. Be specific.

# Chapter 12

New Characters:

**Grace Long:** *a local school teacher in Shalimar and a friend of Susan Byrd's. She flirts with Milkman and steals his watch*

**Lilah:** *cousin of Susan Byrd's who "passes" for white*

**John:** *cousin of Susan Byrd's who "passes" for white*

### *Summary*

Having absorbed the lessons of nature, Milkman forges his identity by pursuing his family history and the origins of his family name.

Milkman goes to see Susan Byrd and finds out that Susan's grandmother, Heddy, is Sing's mother.

Milkman continues to be puzzled over Guitar's attempt on his life.

He marvels over his feeling of "connectedness" with the people of Shalimar: "as though there was some cord or pulse of information they shared." In Michigan, with the exception of Pilate, Milkman felt as if he didn't belong "to any place or anybody."

Guitar confronts Milkman and accuses him of hoarding the gold the two men had agreed to share by secretly shipping it in a crate to Virginia. Guitar compares Milkman to his father because of his greed. Milkman realizes it is useless to try to convince Guitar that the crate Guitar saw Milkman helping a man move at the bus station wasn't a crate of gold. Milkman realizes Guitar will never believe that Milkman was helping a fellow human being because "Guitar had never seen Milkman give anybody a hand, especially a stranger."

Milkman continues to dream about flying, but now the manner of flying is less ostentatious. The flying does not resemble the wings and structure of a powerful airplane, but is the "floating" or "cruising" pose of a man "lying on a couch." Flying is not a man-made form, an airplane, a symbol of modernization, but a form of human transcendence or transformation.

Milkman continues to see the children play the circle-game and sing the song they always sing, but this time he hears a different part of the song. The melody and words of the song are the same as the song that Pilate always sings, but instead of the name "Sugarman," the children sing the name "Solomon."

Milkman is reflective about his relationship with his family members. He experiences a new tenderness for and understanding of his parents. He regrets the feelings of hatred he felt in the past for his sisters. He is especially remorseful about his betrayal of Pilate and his mistreatment of and indifference toward Hagar.

At the end of the chapter, when Milkman determines from the children's song that the "Solomon" they are singing about is his paternal great-grandfather, Milkman "was as eager and as happy as he had ever been in his life."

### Analysis

The sense of community Milkman feels for the people of Shalimar triggers an even deeper interest in Milkman's own family history than he had felt in Danville. Armed with "the sense of lightness and power" his dream about flying has given him, and the fact that "Pilate did not have a navel," Milkman eagerly pursues the answers to his questions: "...why did (Sing) want her husband to keep that awful name? ...To wipe out...his slave past?...And why didn't his own father and Pilate know any of their relatives?"

As Milkman hears the old blues song Pilate always sings about "Sugarman," he is filled with homesickness. Repulsed by his mother in the past, Milkman grows sentimental about her "quiet, crooked, apologetic smile" and sympathizes with her "sexual deprivation." Milkman now possesses the knowledge to be able to understand his father's perversion of Macon Dead I's love for the land: Macon "distorted life, bent it for the sake of gain" because of Macon's profound loss "at his father's death."

Most of all, Milkman is shamed by his betrayal of Pilate in the house that was his sanctuary "without one article of comfort in it, a place where material goods weren't necessary but the things that mattered most—peace," "energy," "singing," and "his own remembrances"—were present. Milkman also admits that he abused

Hagar just to prove that "he was one bad dude, that he had the power to drive a woman out of her mind, to destroy her."

As Milkman is "finding his life" through his reflections, he is losing all his earthly possessions. When he loses his watch to Grace Long, Milkman thinks "All it could do was tell (me) the time of day" and "he really wasn't interested."

At the same time that Milkman is losing his material possessions, Guitar is attempting to make Milkman "lose his life." Unlike Milkman, who has gone through a rite of passage and become a stronger and more complete man because of it, Guitar is slowly being eaten up by his hatred. As Milkman's identity grows and blossoms, Guitar's being has lost its individuality. Guitar has become his cause, and the person behind that cause has been lost.

In the song the children sing about Solomon, Milkman learns part of the history of his family. "Jake the only son of Solomon...whirled about and touched the sun," the song says. From this reference, Milkman determines that Solomon is Jake's father and Milkman's paternal great-grandfather.

The image of Jake, the son of Solomon, touching the sun and falling back to the earth recalls the classical Greek myth of Icarus. Icarus, the son of Daedalus, flew on a pair of artificial wings too close to the sun. When his wings melted, he drowned in the sea.

The biblical Solomon who authored three books of the Bible, was the King of Israel in the tenth century. He was known for his wisdom, wealth, and sense of justice. The name Solomon derives from Shalom, the Hebrew word for peace.

### Study Questions

1. Who does Milkman specifically go to see in Chapter 12 to find out more information about his family? What specifically does he want to know?

2. What is Sing's relationship to Susan Byrd and her father?

3. What is Susan Byrd's grandmother's name?

4. Is it true that it isn't important for Milkman to find his people?

5. What does Milkman realize the ghost is telling Pilate when it says, "Sing"?

6. Since Pilate doesn't have a navel, what else does Milkman figure can also be true?

7. What does Milkman realize he's left behind at Susan Byrd's house?

8. Why does Guitar try to kill Milkman? Why doesn't Guitar believe Milkman's explanation?

9. Why wasn't Milkman really afraid of being killed by Hagar?

10. What does the reference to the "red man's house" in the children's song mean?

## Answers

1. Milkman goes to Susan Byrd's house because he wants to find out about his grandmother, Sing.

2. Sing is Susan Byrd's aunt. Susan Byrd's father, Crowell, Byrd is Sing's brother.

3. Susan Byrd's grandmother is named Heddy Byrd.

4. No, at this point it is important to Milkman to find his people.

5. Milkman realizes the ghost isn't asking Pilate to sing (a song); rather the ghost is saying his wife's name.

6. Because Pilate doesn't have a navel, Milkman figures that it is possible ghosts can exist.

7. Milkman realizes that Grace Long has kept his watch, but he decides that "a watch is not worth worrying about."

8. Guitar tries to kill Milkman because he believes Milkman has recovered the gold and is keeping it for himself. Guitar doesn't believe Milkman's explanation because, as he knows, Milkman never helped anyone in his life.

9. Milkman didn't really believe Hagar would succeed in killing him because of her "weapons" and because of a "complete lack of cunning or intelligence even of conviction, in her attacks."

10. The reference to the "red man's house" in the children's song referred to the Indian heritage of the Byrds.

### Suggested Essay Topics

1. Discuss the encounter between Milkman and Guitar in the chapter. What is the reason for Guitar's lack of faith in Milkman after they have been best friends for so many years? Is this loss of faith believable to you as a reader? Why or why not? Discuss how the Seven Days and Guitar's childhood have influenced the person Guitar has become.

2. Discuss the meaning of Milkman's dream about flying. Compare it to other references to flying in the text. If the significance of flying has changed for Milkman, explain how. Consider flying symbols throughout the novel, and analyze them.

# Chapter 13

New Characters:

**Lilly:** *the owner of Lilly's Beauty Parlor*

**Marcelline:** *an employee of Lilly's Beauty Parlor*

### Summary

Chapter 13 is a flashback to Michigan, and opens with Guitar finding Hagar after she's made her final attempt on Milkman's life. Guitar lectures Hagar on love, telling her "you can't own a human being," and a person "can't value you more than you value yourself." Hagar's love is described as a "stingy little love that ate everything in sight." He blames Pilate and Reba for spoiling her and not giving her the necessary tools to cope in the world outside the home.

Hagar is no longer a functioning human being, and lies comatose in her little "Goldilocks-choice" bed. Finally, when Pilate holds a mirror to her face, Hagar responds with "No wonder." She condemns the face in the mirror that looks back at her. Reba pawns her diamond ring to supply money to buy Hagar all the beauty products she requires to beautify herself. None of the products can make Hagar look "white" enough—the only acceptable standard of beauty she believes will give her the opportunity to lure Milkman back to her. Crushed by this knowledge, Hagar dies of a broken heart.

Ruth shames Macon into giving her money to pay for Hagar's funeral. She is the only family member that attends the service at first. Halfway through the mass, Pilate enters the church singing "Mercy....Mercy?" In singing response, Reba joins her mother as they express the loss of "(their) baby girl."

### *Analysis*

Hagar is representative of the women who "kill for love, die for love." They are women who were "spoiled children," whose every "whim had been taken seriously." They have lacked discipline or any sense of restriction from parents; they've never had to live by the rules imposed by society.

Pilate and Reba are able to create their own worlds and values: Pilate because she is "strong enough," and Reba because she is "simple enough." But Hagar, brought up in a household of unimpeachable freedom that made up its own rules as it went along is ill-equipped to cope in the real world.

Hagar "needed what most colored girls needed: a chorus of mamas, grandmamas, aunts, cousins, sisters, neighbors, Sunday school teachers, best girl friends, and what all to give her the strength life demanded of her—and the humor with which to live it." Pilate and Reba can only love her; they cannot help her to better arm herself to function in the outside world. Both Pilate and Reba are immune to and choose not to live in that world; both wouldn't have the slightest idea how to help Hagar because they are isolated and only function in a limited world.

Without a large enough support group to dispel the corrupt values of the outside world, Hagar is seduced by the rhetoric of advertising ads about beauty. She believes she must look and behave a certain way in order to be loved. Since she perceives Milkman's preference for white features, she strives to achieve such features. Hagar is the ultimate consumer. Hagar purchases cosmetic commodities, and buys into the slogans of her purchases, "read(ing) hungrily the labels and the promises," so that she, too, could "(create) for him a world of tender privacy where the only occupant is you."

Driven by white standards of beauty in society, Hagar is "set up" for failure even before she attempts to change the face she has with "Sunny glow" and "Mango tango." She cannot change her African features into "white" ones. She cannot have "silky hair the color of a penny," or "lemon-colored skin," or "gray-blue eyes." She has no other way to define herself except by her appearance. Therefore, when Hagar is rejected by Milkman, she has nothing else to fall back on. The only love she knows is "nervous love," love as an "affliction."

Guitar uses a metaphor to explain to Hagar how love should be between two people:

> "Did you ever see the way the clouds love a mountain? They circle all around it; sometimes you can't even see the mountains from the clouds. But you know what? You go up top and what do you see? His head. The clouds never cover the head. His head pokes through, because the clouds let him; they don't wrap him up. They let him keep his head up high, free, with nothing to hide him or bind him."

Similes are also used in this chapter:

> "Pilate and Reba, seated beside the bed, bent over her (Hagar) like two divi-divi trees beaten forward by a wind always blowing from the same direction. Like the trees, they offered her all they had: love murmurs and a protective shade."

Milkman reflects on the transforming qualities of life and its ability to metamorphosize from one thing to another, crossing the boundary from the real to the surreal, from the expected to the unexpected. This example combines a collage of concrete images, movie stars images, Walt Disney characters, food, nature, and myth:

> "For a long time now he knew that anything could appear to be something else, and probably was. Nothing could be taken for granted. Women who loved you tried to cut your throat, while women who didn't even know your

name scrubbed your back. Witches could sound like Katherine Hepburn and your best friend could try to strangle you. Smack in the middle of an orchid there might be a blob of jello and inside a Mickey Mouse doll, a fixed radiant star."

### Study Questions

1.  What metaphor does Guitar use to symbolize what love should be like?

2.  Pilate and Reba are credited with being able to "make up (their lives)" each because they have a quality Hagar lacks. What are those qualities?

3.  What happens now when Reba tries to win things?

4.  What facial descriptions are used to describe Pilate and Reba's anxiety over Hagar's condition?

5.  What does Reba pawn in order to get Hagar the necessary money for her shopping trip? How much money does Hagar take with her to shop?

6.  Why does Marcelline of Lilly's Beauty Parlor agree to take Hagar as a customer in spite of the late hour?

7.  What happens to Hagar's shopping bags on the way home?

8.  What happens after Hagar dresses up and presents herself to Pilate and Reba and sees herself in their eyes?

9.  Who pays for Hagar's funeral and why? What lone member of the Macon Dead family attends?

10. What three words does Pilate repeat to refer to Hagar at the funeral mass?

### Answers

1.  Guitar uses the metaphor "the way the clouds love a mountain" to explain to Hagar how love should be.

2.  Pilate is "strong enough" and Reba is "simple enough," Hagar is neither.

3. When Reba tries to win things, for the first time in her life, she is unable to.

4. Pilate's lips are described as "still." Reba's eyes are described as "full of panic" to exhibit their anxiety over Hagar's condition.

5. Reba pawns her diamond ring to get Hagar money to shop. Hagar goes shopping with $200.75.

6. Marcelline agrees to take Hagar as a customer at the Beauty Parlor because she is afraid Hagar or Pilate might be dangerous.

7. Hagar's shopping bags split because it is raining.

8. After Hagar realizes how she must appear, she cries for hours and then develops a fever.

9. Macon Dead pays for Hagar's funeral at the insistence of his wife, Ruth. Ruth is the only member of the Macon Dead family to attend the funeral.

10. Pilate calls Hagar "my baby girl" at the funeral mass.

### Suggested Essay Topics

1. Consider Guitar's advice to Hagar. Is he a sympathetic character in this chapter? If you believe he is, consider what character traits make him sympathetic. How do these character traits compare with your other impressions of Guitar throughout the novel? Compare and contrast them.

2. Discuss how society's standards influence how we think about ourselves. How is Hagar a victim of these standards? How are both black and white women victims of standards of beauty? Is there one "true" model of beauty for white women? Discuss standards of beauty in different cultures. Consider whether men are also victims of standards of beauty.

# Chapter 14

## *Summary*

Milkman returns to Susan Byrd's house, hopeful that she can further enlighten him about his family history after he has decoded the children's song about Solomon. Susan fills in the gaps about Sing and Jake's relationship and tells Milkman Jake was one of Solomon's (or Shalimar's) children; the names are synonymous. Susan also tells Milkman about the tale of the flying African: according to the legend, before witnesses Solomon flew off "like a bird" back to Africa to escape slavery, leaving his grieving wife Ryna and 21 sons behind, although he had tried to take Jake, his youngest, with him.

## *Analysis*

Chapter 14 features a conversation between Susan Byrd and Milkman which helps to assemble the final pieces of the Dead family puzzle.

Of the greatest significance in the chapter is Milkman's revelation that his paternal great-grandfather Solomon could fly and that the town of Shalimar is the very home his family originated from. Unbeknownst to him, Milkman has been in the town of his origins the entire time he has been unraveling the mystery behind his family name and history.

The flying motif that has structured the novel reaches its near-conclusion. For Milkman, flight, which had been a possibility before the age of four, has again become a possibility. If Macon Dead I can appear as a ghost and Pilate can have no navel, then flight, too, can be a reality.

Milkman's first revelation was his discovery of his "authentic" self, while he was only "breath" and "thoughts" in the darkness of the hunting grounds near Solomon's Leap and Ryna's Gulch. His identity, however, lacked wholeness and a sense of completion without the knowledge of his family name and the place of their origin. Now with these two mysteries solved and the knowledge that Solomon was a flying African, Milkman cannot wait to return to Michigan to bring the message home.

### Study Questions

1. Why doesn't Susan Byrd tell Milkman the truth about his family in front of Grace Long?

2. According to Susan Byrd, what is Jake's last name?

3. Who did Solomon leave behind when he flew back to Africa?

4. Approximately how many families consider themselves the kin of Solomon in the town of Shalimar?

5. What place besides the town is named after Solomon? What is its significance?

6. What other reason does Susan Byrd give to explain why Ryna lost her mind besides the reason of "love"?

7. How does Susan Byrd explain to Milkman why the children's song says, "Jake the only son of Solomon?

8. Who took care of Jake after he slipped out of Solomon's arms as Solomon flew back to Africa?

9. Why did Jake have to register at the Freedmen's Bureau?

10. What does Milkman say when Susan Byrd offers to get Milkman's watch back?

### Answers

1. Susan Byrd doesn't tell the truth in front of Grace Long because Grace is a "gossip."

2. Susan Byrd tells Milkman that Jake didn't have a last name because he is "one of those flying African children."

3. Solomon left his wife, Ryna, and 21 children behind when he flew back to Africa.

4. More than 40 families in the area consider themselves Solomon's kin.

5. A big double-headed rock over the valley is named after Solomon because it's where Solomon took flight to Africa. It's called Solomon's Leap.

6.  Besides love, Susan Byrd reasons that Ryna must have lost her mind because she had 21 children to care for by herself.

7.  Susan believes that the song says "Jake the only son of "Solomon" because Jake was the one Solomon was trying to take with him when he flew back to Africa.

8.  Heddy, Sing's mother, took Jake into her home after Jake slipped out of Solomon's arms and fell to the ground.

9.  Jake had to register at the Freedmen's Bureau because he had been a slave.

10. When Susan Byrd offers to get Milkman's watch back from Grace Long, Milkman tells her "never mind."

### Suggested Essay Topics

1.  Discuss the reasons Susan Byrd didn't tell Milkman the truth about his family when Grace Long was present. Is Susan's concern with the gossip based on racism or not? Discuss the narrator's point of view on intermarriage between Indians and blacks.

2.  Reconstruct a brief genealogical history of the Dead family. Explain how oral history has kept the Dead past alive. Consider all the characters that have contributed stories to this history.

# Chapter 15

### Summary

Elated by his discovery of the story of the flying African, Milkman shares his exultation with Sweet by frolicking joyfully in the waters of Shalimar while yelling at the top of his lungs "my great-granddaddy could flyyyyyy and the whole damn town is named after him."

On his return trip to Michigan, Milkman reads the road signs with interest and wonders "what lay beneath the names." Milkman knows that "under the recorded names were other names, just as 'Macon Dead,' recorded for all time in some dusty file, hid from

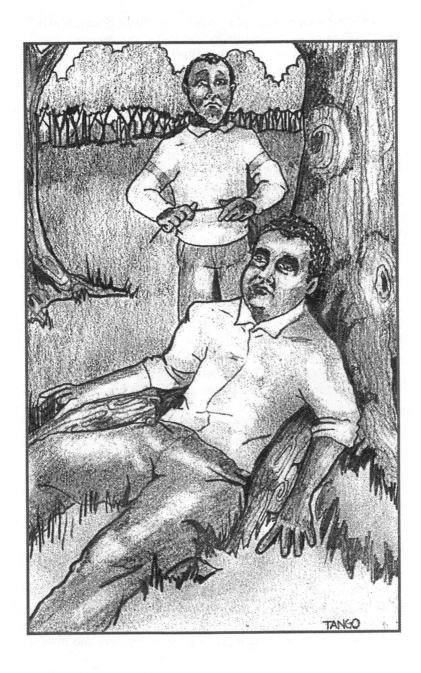

view the real names of people, places, and things. Names that had meaning"—names whose history was lost with their erasure.

Upon arriving in Michigan, Milkman hastens off to Pilate's house to tell her that the green sack she's been carrying is filled with the bones of her father. Milkman also wants to tell her that the ghost of her father wasn't telling her to sing; he was calling out her mother's name. Instead, when Milkman arrives, Pilate "knocks him out" and puts him in the basement next to a shoe box filled with Hagar's hair. Milkman realizes that "while he dreamt of flying, Hagar was dying." It reminds him of his great-grandfather Solomon, leaving Ryna behind. Milkman explains to Pilate the meaning of the words "You just can't fly on off and leave a body." Milkman tells Pilate that her father wants her to bury him in Virginia, at Solomon's Leap "where he belongs."

As Pilate and Milkman prepare to bury Macon Dead I (or Jake), the smell of ginger permeates the air. Instead of putting a rock or cross on the grave, Pilate yanks off her earring "with the single word Jake ever wrote" on it and puts it in his grave. A concealed Guitar shoots Pilate, and she dies as Milkman, at her request, sings her into death. Milkman realizes he loves her because "she could fly...without ever leaving the ground." Yelling to Guitar, "You want my life? You need it?" Milkman turns toward Guitar and leaps into the air, surrendering to "the killing arms of his brother." Like the mythic Greek hero, Milkman returns to the bosom of his family to share his new-found knowledge.

### Analysis

As *Song of Solomon* concludes, the themes of the novel resurface to frame the text, as they did in the beginning of the novel. At the onset of Chapter 1, Pilate sings to soothe Ruth, as pregnant with Milkman, she goes into premature labor. As the novel ends, Milkman sings, sending Pilate off into the final phase of the life cycle—the death phase. But Pilate's death is a form of rebirth because in cyclical time, as one phase ends, another begins.

As Milkman speaks the words to the old blues song Pilate sang at his birth, he links the past—the song of Solomon, and the song of Sugarman—with the present, the song of Sugargirl. The song embraces both the oral tradition of song as memory and history, and naming. And once again, the song is accompanied by flight. First, as Pilate is lain to rest, a bird flies off with her earring, carrying her name and her spirit back to Africa. Then Milkman, who has acquired the knowledge to "sing his aunt off," follows her, as his "pilot" takes her last journey, leading him to his final destination.

Armed with the knowledge he has acquired from the lessons of his family history and naming, Milkman realizes what is necessary for flight. The key to flying is not trying to master the air the way an airplane does; the key is to surrender yourself to the air. Once Milkman realizes that, he learns flying is as natural as breathing.

Ocean and water motifs are found in Milkman's desperate need to swim in the ocean, a delayed reaction to the feeling of being landlocked in Chapter 7. Milkman is ecstatic and feels he is on the verge of something—the actualization of flight.

The ocean is a symbol of "universal life," of "ceaseless movement,", and it is "the source of the generation of all life." (The Dictionary of Symbols, Cirlot, 230)

For Milkman to submerge himself in water, even if it is not in the sea, is not only a cleansing act, but it is a regenerative act. Earlier, Milkman washed off his shame in the bathtub, but in this instance, the washing of himself in the waters of nature has much greater moral consequences. It is a joyful baptism, in anticipation of a new self that embraces life. This cleansing is a final step before flight.

The following sense impression also appear in this chapter: "A deep sigh escaped from the sack and the wind turned chill. Ginger, a spicy sugared smell, enveloped them." At the moment of Jake's release, the air is permeated with the scent of ginger. Ginger continues to be associated with memory, the past, and the flight back home to Africa.

### Study Questions

1. Where does Milkman want to swim?

2. Once Sweet learns that Solomon flew back to Africa, what is her next question? Why?

3.  Why does Milkman read the road signs "with interest" on his ride back to Michigan?

4.  What is the official name of "Not Doctor" street? Why isn't it used?

5.  Why doesn't the narrator include a list of names in the last chapter?

6.  What does Milkman conclude that all human relationships "boil down to"?

7.  What does Pilate do when, upon Milkman's return, he tries to embrace her?

8.  Where is the "something of Hagar's" that Pilate has put near Milkman in the cellar?

9.  Why didn't Milkman and Pilate fly to Virginia when they traveled there to bury Jake's bones?

10. What does Pilate put on the grave instead of a rock or a cross?

### Answers

1.  Milkman wants to swim in the sea.

2.  Sweet's second question is about whom Solomon left behind. As a woman she is concerned with the welfare of the women and children.

3.  Milkman reads the road signs with interest because he knows that beneath the names of the signs are other buried names that have meaning.

4.  The official name of "Not Doctor" street is Mains Avenue, but the black community doesn't use it because it has no meaning or history for the people who live there.

5.  The narrator includes a list of names that bears witness to a past. Through the names the past can be recalled and memorialized. The list of names also celebrates both the fictitious figures of *Song of Solomon* and the historic figures and referents in African American history.

6.  Milkman concludes that all human relationships boil down to: "Would you save my life? Or would you take it?"

7.  When Milkman tries to embrace Pilate after his return from Michigan, she breaks a "wet green bottle over his head."

8.  Pilate has put Hagar's hair in a shoe box near to Milkman.

9.  Milkman and Pilate don't fly to Virginia because Pilate will not "step foot on an airplane."

10. Pilate put her earring in the grave, instead of putting a rock or cross on it.

### Suggested Essay Topics

1.  Discuss the theme of flying with regard to those who are left behind. Is it always the men who "fly off" and the women and children who are left behind? Consider male responsibility to family in your discussion. Draw on your own experiences. Do you think the narrator, in *Song of Solomon,* takes a stand on this issue? Cite examples in the text.

2.  Consider Pilate's behavior in the final chapter. What makes her a simple and what makes her a complex character. Discuss her belief system and how it influences her behavior. Do you think she is a believable character? Does it matter whether she is believable? Why or why not? Why does Milkman say, at the end of the book, that "without ever leaving the ground, (Pilate) could fly?" Explain what Milkman means.

# SECTION THREE

# *Sample Analytical Paper Topics*

The following paper topics are designed to test your understanding of the novel by giving you the opportunity to analyze some of the important themes of *Song of Solomon*. Following each topic is a sample outline to help direct you to the main points of the topic and to encourage your own ideas.

### Topic #1

Milkman goes through several stages in the growing-up process to become a humane and morally-responsible adult. Discuss the most significant turning points in his march toward manhood in *Song of Solomon*. Explain their impact on Milkman's character.

### Outline

I.  Thesis Statement: *Milkman's progress in becoming a morally-responsible and humane character in* Song of Solomon *is primarily a result of his becoming educated in his family's past, in his understanding of nature, and in his new-found respect for women.*

II. Learning about his family's past

    A.  Pilate's values as an alternative to Macon's

    B.  Milkman's father did not always have such values

    C.  His grandfather Jake's importance to the Shalimar community

      D.   Finds out Solomon was a flying African

III.   Learning from nature

      A.   Material possessions are useless in nature

      B.   Man cannot control nature

      C.   Nature can overpower man

      D.   Man can communicate with and learn about living from nature

IV.   Learning about women

      A.   Learns Ruth and his sisters are not subservient to men, and do not exist only to nurture men

      B.   Hagar and other women do not exist solely for his physical pleasure

      C.   Pilate and Circe (and to a lesser extent, Reba) do not fit in "traditional" gender categories

      D.   Sweet is Milkman's first reciprocal relationship

### Topic #2

There are essentially three types of women in *Song of Solomon*. The Macon Dead family women (Ruth, Lena, and Corinthians) live in the domestic realm where they are oppressed by men. Pilate, Circe, and to a lesser extent Reba, live in a mythic world of their own making where they are essentialy self-sufficient. The impressionable Hagar exists in the gap between these two worlds and is ill at ease in both. Compare and contrast these three types of women and the worlds they inhabit.

### Outline

I.    Thesis statement: *Compare and contrast the three types of women in* Song of Solomon *and the worlds they inhabit. Compare the domestic realm of Ruth and her daughters, the mythic realm of Pilate, Circe, and Reba, and the consumer-oriented realm that Hagar inhabits.*

II.   Domestic realm (Ruth, Lena, Corinthians)

A. Function as domestics in the household

B. Are inferiors to and serve men

C. Have no independent existences throughout most of the novel; dependent on men

D. Cultivate nature to compensate for life-denying existences symbolized by the artificial rose petals

    1. Ruth's flowers and goldfish; Ruth's garden in Milkman's dream

    2. Lena's maple tree

III. Mythic realm (Pilate, Circe, Reba)

A. Create own rules and codes of behavior

B. Are conjurers or sage-like, use incantations and folk remedies

C. Are not male-dependent

D. Act from a source of power and are in sync with nature

IV. Consumer-oriented realm (Hagar)

A. Struggles in gap betwen Pilate and Ruth's world

B. Lacks support group to determine what is of value

C. Has a perverted sense of self

D. Dependent on a white standard of beauty as basis for self-worth; male-dependent

### Topic #3

Consider the circumstances that contribute to the change in Guitar Bains' character. How was he scarred in his childhood to such a degree that at one point in the novel he says, "Fair is one more thing I've given up"?

### Outline

I. Thesis Statement: *Guitar Bain's character changes from a living, breathing human being to one who lives for an ideal. Consider how his childhood conflicts, the death of his father and the aftermath, contribute to his adult biases.*

II.  Childhood conflicts

A.  Father killed when Guitar was four years old

B.  Mother accepts payoff from white sawmill owner

   1.  Four ten-dollar bills

   2.  Divinity candy

C.  Mother cannot cope with husband's loss and runs away

D.  Guitar avoids relationships because everything he ever loved died

III.  Adult Biases

A.  Respect for nature (life of a doe) changes to lack of respect: does not value human life

B.  Joins Seven Days and judges people based on their skin color

C.  Eventually ceases to trust even Milkman

D.  Calls association with Seven Days an "act of love" as he hones ability to kill

# SECTION FOUR

# *Bibliography*

Quotations from *Song of Solomon* are taken from the following edition:

Morrison, Toni. *Song of Solomon.* New York: New American Library, 1977.

***Other sources:***

Appiah, K.A. and Gates Jr., Henry Louis, eds. *Toni Morrison: Critical Perspectives Past and Present.* New York: Amistad, 1993.

Campbell, Joseph. *The Hero with a Thousand Faces.* London: Abacus, 1975.

Carmean, Karen. *Toni Morrison's World of Fiction.* Troy, New York: The Whitston Publishing Co., 1993.

Century, Douglas. *Toni Morrison.* New York: Chelsea House Publishing, 1994.

Cirlot, J.E. *A Dictionary of Symbols.* New York: Philosophical Library, 1962.

Dematrakopoulos, Stephanie A. and Holloway, Karla F. C. *New Dimensions of Spirituality—A Biracial and Bicultural Reading of the Novels of Toni Morrison.* New York: Greenwood Press, 1987.

Harris, Trudier. *Fiction and Folklore: The Novels of Toni Morrison.* Knoxville: University of Tennessee Press, 1991.

Lardner, Susan. "Word of Mouth," *The New Yorker,* November 7, 1977, 217–221.

LeClair, Thomas. "'The Language Must Not Sweat': A Conversation with Toni Morrison," *New Republic*, March 21, 1981, 25–29.

Mbalia, Doreatha Drummond. *Toni Morrison's Developing Class Consciousness*. Selinsgrove: Susquehanna University Press, London and Toronto: Associated University Presses, 1991.

McKay, Nellie Y. *Critical Essays on Toni Morrison*. Boston: G.K. Hall and Co., 1988.

Millar, Neil. "Toni Morrison's Brilliant Black Novel," *Christian Science Monitor*, October 20, 1977, 25.

Morrison, Toni. "Toni Morrison on the 'Spoken Library,'" (Excerpt of speech at the NCTE Annual Convention). *English Journal*, February, 1978, 29.

Strouse, Jean. "Toni Morrison's Black Magic," *Newsweek*, March 30, 1981, 52–57.

Walker, Melissa. *Down From the Mountaintio: Black Wopmen's Novels in the Wake of the Civil Rights Movement (1966–1989)*. New Haven: Yale University Press, 1991.

Wigan, Angela. "Native Daughter," *Time*, September 12, 1977, 76.

THE BEST TEST PREPARATION FOR THE

# AP
## ADVANCED
## PLACEMENT
## EXAMINATION

# ENGLISH
## Literature & Composition

by Pauline Beard, Ph.D. • Robert Liftig, Ed.D. • James Malek, Ph.D. •
James Maloney, M.A. • Joanne Miller, M.A. • Peter Trenouth, M.A. • Mottie Williams, M.A.

## 6 Full-Length Exams

➤ Every question based on the current exams
➤ The ONLY test preparation book with detailed explanations to every question
➤ Far more comprehensive than any other test preparation book

Includes a COMPREHENSIVE AP COURSE REVIEW,
emphasizing all areas of literature & composition found on the exam

**REA** *Research & Education Association*

*Available at your local bookstore or order directly from us by sending in coupon below.*